MUSIC TO MY EARS

Testimonials

"I finished *Peace Dreamer* with tears of joy for having the honor of reading this powerful, profound and personal book of wisdom. Cheryl Melody Baskin is the new Mr. Rogers. She is one of the most evolved souls in our world and her loving way of relating to the reader will bathe you in possibilities and nourish your soul. All her words of comfort come from her brilliant understanding of our struggles. As she said, "I wanted every word on every page to come from an authentic place deep within my soul, and I wanted to give you hope amid all the chaos." She does that skillfully as she integrates her personal experiences with insights that help us understand ourselves, and at the same time, igniting our dreams for peace. She has given us a roadmap for personal renewal that will create our tomorrows with heart-led purpose for the peaceful future our world needs today!"

> – **Barbara Gaughen-Muller**, Co-founder and President: www.RotaryEclubofWorldPeace.org; President of the United Nations Association – Santa Barbara, www.unasb.org; Peace Podcast host: www.PeacePodcast.org

"*Peace Dreamer* is that rare book written with love for the entire world and everyone in it. Author, Cheryl Melody Baskin, has gifted readers with a book that expresses her desire that all people feel love, acceptance and inner peace. She gently encourages readers to examine our values and innermost feelings, including our biases and prejudices. She urges us to be courageous and persistent in our quest to understand how our own life experiences have shaped us. More importantly, she provides the tools to make it possible. Throughout this book, she helps us figure out how each of us can bring more peace and love into our own lives and into the world we all share. Ultimately, this book is an offering of hope and empowerment for all who read it."

> – **Jan Krause Greene**, Author of *I Call Myself Earth Girl; What Happens in the Space Between* and *Left for Dead: From Surviving to Thriving.* www.jkgreene.com

"Cheryl Melody Baskin has created a book that can be used as powerful life coaching. I see *Peace Dreamer* as a means by which wounded souls can be reparented and reborn to a life filled with love and hope. Life is difficult, but it is also possible to turn a curse into a blessing and find the open door you thought didn't exist. Let this book be your guide to finding your true and joyful new life."

> – **Bernie S. Siegel, M.D.**, Author of *Love, Medicine & Miracles, Peace Love & Healing, No Endings, Only Beginnings* and *365 Prescriptions for the Soul.* www.berniesiegelmd.com

"Cheryl Melody Baskin has written a book that is perfect for our times. It is a poetic treatise that provides hope, insight and wisdom that successfully addresses the profound difficulties in our society. Cheryl speaks from the depths of her soul and shows us how to overcome doubt and fear by uncovering the goodness within each of us. This book is not only heartwarming but is a necessary guide to overcoming the stressful times we all currently face. Be good to yourself and read this book slowly, integrate every section into your psyche and you will likely grow and thrive."

> – **Arthur P. Ciaramicoli**, Ed.D., Ph.D., Clinical
> psychologist and author of *The Triumph of Diversity* and
> *The Soulful Leader*. www.balanceyoursuccess.com

"Cheryl Melody Baskin's latest work, *Peace Dreamer*, provides a much-needed sense of hope amidst all the chaos of today's pandemic-infused, politically charged world. May her actionable tools, strategies, and wisdom to "never give up, no matter how messy life becomes," guide and uplift you. Baskin believes we have the power to be the soul of peace and love, even during the darkest times. *Peace Dreamer* will help you keep your eyes on the horizon, live inspired and BE the peace you seek."

> – **Deborah Burke Henderson**, Writer, public relations
> professional, and creator of the nationally recognized,
> "Wednesday's Child" television series

"Peace Dreamer: A Journey of Hope in Bad Times and Good is a salve for the soul. In a world that has been plagued by disease, racial injustice, violence and discord, Cheryl Melody Baskin, divinely and poetically prescribes an elixir for peace. She reminds us that all our dreams are attainable when we tap into the trove of ourselves. Throughout, Baskin provides us with the navigational tools for inner and outer peace. What a gift!"

> – **Liseli A. Fitzpatrick, Ph.D.**, Trinidadian poet and professor of African Cosmologies and Sacred Ontologies, Wellesley College, Massachusetts. www.wellesley.edu/africana/faculty/fitzpatrick

"What a refreshing, inspiring book, and what a time for this book to emerge! I am so grateful for Melody's open heart and her honesty. She acknowledges her own struggles in a way that helps me acknowledge my own, but she doesn't stay stuck there, and she doesn't let me stay stuck either. Gently and persistently, she invites us to choose hope and to trust that we are part of a larger spirit of healing. I love that she gives us practical, manageable ways to make a shift in our hearts and our lives. I especially appreciate the list of affirmations and her accessible and simple chakra meditations."

> – **Reverend Dr. Deborah L. Clark**, Author of *Ice Cream at the Ashram; Holy Journey, Holy River, Holy Week*; Pastor at Edwards Church, UCC; Multi-faith coordinator for Open Spirit. www.openspiritcenter.org

Dedication

Peace Dreamer is dedicated to Justice Ruth Bader Ginsburg

May we all be warriors. Warriors on behalf of justice, equality, human rights, fairness, truth, integrity, tenacity, wisdom, courage, optimism, strength, dignity, determination, persistence, resilience, compassion, kindness and unconditional love. Let's embody "RBG's" unstoppable energy, positive core values and her resolute dream for a respectful and inclusive world.

Peace Dreamer is also dedicated to all peacebuilders, changemakers, lightworkers, peace visionaries, on-the-fence doubters, heart-dreamers, optimists, creative thinkers, healers, thought leaders, truth seekers, perfectly imperfect human beings and soul-searchers.

Peace Dreamer

A Journey of Hope in Bad Times and Good

Cheryl Melody Baskin

Library of Congress Cataloging-in-Publication Data
Library of Congress Control Number: 2020924351

Baskin, Cheryl Melody
Peace Dreamer: A Journey of Hope in Bad Times and Good
Cheryl Melody Baskin

Paperback ISBN 978-1-7333681-5-5
eBook ISBN 978-1-7333681-6-2

Cover and interior by YellowStudios LLC (www.YellowStudiosOnline.com)

Categories: self-help   spiritual growth   personal transformation
              inspirational/motivational   human rights

Printed in the United States of America

CONTENTS

Preface

Dear Friend,

Thank you for inviting *Peace Dreamer* into your home and heart. My book of hope was written from the part of my soul that believes in the goodness of people and our ability to change, heal and grow. I have faith that we have the power to find common ground amid adversity, shift from fear to love, and embody the core values of kindness, compassion, empathy and respect. I will always envision the possibility of living in a world of peace, diversity celebration and love, no matter what.

It wasn't easy to write a book like this in the middle of a pandemic. It also wasn't easy to write a book like this during an intense period of social, racial and political polarization. There were days when I experienced brain fog, anxiety, fear and exhaustion. Typically, I am an intense keep-my-nose-to-the-grindstone-until-my-project-is-done kind of person. This time, I couldn't even try to "push the river," which rarely works anyway. As much as I wanted to publish my heartfelt thoughts as quickly as possible, I needed to take my time, let go, and surrender to the timetable of the universe. Before I could share my heart with you from a place of truth and clarity, I needed to center myself first.

I turned to my favorite self-care tools, listened to my inner rhythms, and respected the whispers of my highest intuition. I would ask myself, "Is today a good day to write my book and share my heart, wisdom, personal experiences, experiential activities, and out-of-the-box thinking?"

You see, I wanted every word on every page to come from an authentic place deep within my soul, and I wanted to give you hope amid all the chaos. Above all, I wanted to stand by your side as a new friend and urge you to never give up, no matter how messy life becomes.

As I wrote *Peace Dreamer*, I had you in my mind and heart. I wondered, "How are you feeling? What are your many life stories? How have they influenced your thoughts on peace, love and hope? Who is this beautiful person?" We may not have met, but I know that I am not alone with my dreams and doubts, weaknesses and strengths, fears and resilience, courage and exhaustion. I also know that I'm not alone in believing that we have power to be the soul of peace even during the darkest times. When we use peace as a verb, its meaning is simple. Kindness, compassion, forgiveness, an open heart, an open mind, self-reflection, empathy, helping each other in times of need, a warm smile, manners, and an intention of the heart and to the heart to reach beyond all borders and differences.

We all have dreams for a better world. Some of us express our desires by quietly meditating, writing, praying, singing, visualizing and living the essence of peace and love. Others belong to a community of like-minded people who believe in the same values. Many changemakers enjoy both forms of support and expression.

Whichever path you choose, never give up, my friend. Peace is possible. Love is possible. Justice is possible. Unity is possible. Compassion is possible. Kindness is possible. Empathy is possible. Respect is possible. Forgiveness is possible. Healing is possible. Hope is possible.

Peace Dreamer is here to inspire you to keep your eyes up on the horizon, use love and peace as your compass, and continually feed your spirit with grand dreams, endless possibilities, child-like wonder, an open heart, idealism, optimism, open-minded curiosity, positive action and hope.

One last thing. This is also a book that lends itself to looking within, self-discovery and personal transformation. It asks you, "What are your core values? What do you believe? Is there a way to offer even more of your innate gifts, energy and love to others? What kind of world do you hope to leave behind?"

Most of all, thank you. Thank you for opening your mind and heart to *Peace Dreamer*. Thank you for joining me in my desire to create one global community of love.

From my heart to yours,

Melody

CHAPTER ONE

The Dream

"Every great dream begins with a dreamer. Always remember, you have within you the strength, the patience, and the passion to reach for the stars to change the world."

– Harriet Tubman

The Gift That Changed My Life Forever

"The fact that I can plant a seed and it becomes a
flower, share a bit of knowledge and it becomes
another's, smile at someone and receive a smile in
return, are to me continual spiritual exercises."

—Leo Buscaglia, Ph.D.

I was fifteen. Shy. Introspective. Creative. Scarred by the
ramifications of religious discrimination and bullying. Delighted
by nature, music, peace, and the goodness in people. Loved
singing and playing the cello. Happy to live in the beautiful state
of Vermont. Created plays and stories in my imagination long
into the night. Sensitive. Heart-centered. Empathic. Trusting.
Innocent. A dreamer. Idealistic. Imaginative. Felt invisible.

Like many teenagers, I was a mix of confusing personality traits
and emotions. That's when I met Morris. Typically, when my
parents wanted me to meet one of their friends, I was dutiful,
polite, shy and detached. This time, it was different. Given the
wide age span between us, it was difficult to understand why
we seemed to connect on a deep soul-to-soul level, but we did.
Not only was Morris a philosopher, doctor, professor, poet,
mystic, artist and musician, but he was also warm, personable
and eager to share his wisdom.

Every day for a week, we spent an hour of quality time
exchanging our deepest thoughts, questions and feelings. We
talked about the soul, our dream for peace in the world, our

personal definitions of God, spirituality, religion, fear, love, compassion, the innate gifts we've been given, and the healing power of nature. As we communicated, I felt honored to be seen, heard and validated at a time when I often felt invisible, and because of our dynamic conversations, the trajectory of my life and the way I saw myself shifted.

> *Morris saw more light in me than I could see in myself, and because of his faith in me, I began to place that light into my heart and dream of ways that I could help the world become a more loving and inclusive place.*

Our conversations felt like a soothing massage to my spirit, and fifty years later, his words continue to resonate deep within my soul. In fact, my personal and professional choices have been guided by them.

> *"Don't hide your gifts, Melody. You were given unique gifts for a reason. Don't shrivel your-self up and make yourself small. Shine your light. Become the heart of peace. Do your part to bring more love into the world."*

Morris validated my essence, encouraged my innate talents to flourish, urged me to continue to ask the universe deep questions, and showed me countless ways to invite the inner spaciousness required to hear life's highest guidance.

When I'm feeling discouraged about the state of our world, I turn to the imprinted auditory memory of Morris's words passionately advocating that my thoughts turn towards life's miracles and possibilities.

> *Imagine! One person did all that! He would look me straight in the eyes, smile warmly, open his heart, offer his full attention and presence, listen deeply, suspend judgment, share his wisdom, and radiate love. In short, he was the essence of the mantra, "peace begins with me."*

Life Wisdom: Everyone holds a beautiful piece of Morris in their soul. It is not necessary to have a college education to share what we have learned in life. We don't need to be an author, poet, doctor, philosopher or mystic. We can step boldly into our own magnificence and become an inspirational light that changes someone's life forever. It only takes one person to inspire one life and I have a feeling that you're the one for the job. As they say in Hollywood, you've got the "IT" factor. Share your life lessons and learned wisdom with others, and in the process, a part of you may heal, too. How can you resist this idea? It's a win-win.

Never Give Up

"Each note is a need coming through one of us, a passion, a longing pain. Remember the Lips where the wind-breath originated, and let your note be clear. Don't try to end it. BE your note."

– Rumi

Loving consciousness. Finding common ground. Inclusion. Unity. Diversity celebration. Understanding. Justice. Freedom. Healing. Determination. Strength. Courage. Integrity. Truth. Wisdom. Empathy. Harmony. Reverence. Resilience. Possibility. Collective Consciousness. Emotional elasticity. Open dialogue. Listening. Social Responsibility. Joy. Creativity. Humility. Optimism. Cooperation. Respect. Kindness. Mindfulness. Forgiveness. Collaboration. Authenticity. Compassion. Gratefulness. Grace. Faith. Trust. Inspiration. Happiness. Love. Peace. Hope.

There is such magnificence and power in these words, and they inspire me to shout from the rooftops, **YES!** *This* is the kind of world I yearn to create with others. Join me as lightworkers, healers, peacebuilders, creative thinkers, heart-dreamers, optimists, on-the-fence doubters, thought leaders, truth seekers, peace visionaries, soul-searchers, perfectly imperfect human beings and changemakers as we work together to propel the energy of peace and love into the world.

As the poet, Rumi said, "*BE* your note." Each action that shines love and stands for love is all that is needed to create a compassionate and inclusive world. The time is now to elevate humanity to a new awakening, and every positive thought, word, feeling, action and reaction can bring us closer to the kind of world we envision.

The desire to be a catalyst for love and peace is not for the faint-hearted. It takes unwavering focus, self-belief, faith, trust, persistence and courage. There are times when my heart breaks as I witness a world plagued with the negative energy of violence, discrimination, political polarization, complicit silence, inhumanity, inequality, and a general lack of human decency. I find myself thinking, "Wait a minute. Loving consciousness? Peace? I wonder if peace is even possible. Besides, I'm not Ruth Bader Ginsberg or Gandhi."

If you have moments of doubt, please know in your heart that even optimists, idealists and changemakers get discouraged. It's normal. We're human. Acknowledge your feelings, shake them off, take long, slow and deep breaths, order the voice of self-doubt to fly far away on another planet somewhere, and give yourself an inspirational pep talk.

> *Reaffirm your focused archer-with-a-bow dreams and continue to work tirelessly towards a world in which we can all be proud. Never give up. Stay the course. Focus on values that elevate and uplift the human soul and embody the essence of love.*

No. I am not Ruth Bader Ginsberg and I am not Gandhi. *I am me.* I believe in a world that celebrates the diversity of all its global citizens and I see everyone through the heart of love. I am committed to spreading love wherever I go, and until the last breath, I am unstoppable towards this quest.

When I think of all the millions of people around the globe who believe in peace, diversity celebration and love, I am inspired beyond all adequate words. They are ordinary people who are also extraordinary. They embody what it means to be a *Peace Dreamer,* and most of all, they remind me that I am not alone in my own dream.

Think of all the peace dreamers in history who have inspired you with their courage, vision and actions. Think of all the peace dreamers who are actively working towards a world of higher consciousness. Who are your mentors and role models? Breathe in their energy, passion, hope, determined actions, persistence and courage and let them inspire your own passion for living in a world of peace.

> *The dream for inner peace and peace in our world begins with a thought, a small seed, an intention, a hope, and a small or big action step. The longing stirs inside the heart of every Peace Dreamer. The dream begins with me. The dream begins with you.*

Life Wisdom: As we work to resolve the many injustices that plague our planet, it is equally important to focus on healing the wounds that plague our own soul, too. The saying, "peace begins with me," rings true. There is a strong spiritual connection between inner healing and the healing of our planet. Each is dependent on the other. As we transform for the better, so does the world. It is exciting to realize the power and magnitude of inner growth, and it is important to do everything we can to create an alignment between both worlds.

I often ask myself, "Are all my actions, words, feelings and thoughts aligned with my core value of love?"

As soon as I ask this question, a spotlight of positive intention is aimed toward achieving congruency between peace in my own soul, peace for my family and friends, and peace in the world. Continue to work on healing yourself. Continue to connect with like-minded people who believe in similar causes. Work on issues you care about most, use the creative arts as a tool for changing the consciousness of the world, step into local and national leadership positions, be mindful of the influential and positive power of your words, thoughts, feelings, actions and reactions, and meditate in the form of quiet prayer, visualization, positive thought transference, writing, and the healing power of sound.

> *Join me in being the love, compassion and kindness we envision for our world. Join me in being a light that shines towards peace. Never give up on our collective dream. Step by step, resolve to do the inner work needed to heal yourself, and breath by breath, visualize a world that stands tall for peace, justice, inclusion and love.*

Inner Inquiry and
Personal Transformation

"Look within. The answers that you are seeking from
someone else are all inside you. You are your own
inner guru and guide. Listen to the wisdom whispers
of the universe. Follow your heart, highest wisdom,
intuition, and inner voice. Listen."

– Cheryl Melody Baskin

Even when I was young, I tended to look within and ask
deep introspective questions. In the opening chapter of *Peace
Dreamer*, I shared my story about Morris. When I met him
at fifteen, he inspired me to continue my journey of inner
inquiry. We intuitively knew that it was a key towards self-
discovery, transformation, personal growth, healing, clarity and
mindfulness.

Each transformational change begins by asking ourselves a
question. In fact, many questions. Throughout this book of
hope, there will be many opportunities for you to look within
and rediscover your core beliefs, values, dreams, goals and
action plans. The art of inner inquiry encourages us to ask
soul-searching questions, listen to the wisdom whispers of
the universe, and greet ourselves with new layers of self-
understanding. Transformational questioning inspires inner
curiosity and the quest to dream bigger dreams for ourselves
and for the world. It helps us grow, discover our innermost

truth, make conscious choices, shift our perspectives, open our hearts, and discern which issues stir our souls.

My soul-searching questions of the day. On one of my contemplative walks, I asked myself a stream of questions that had been rattling around in my soul ...

> *What does "living in a democracy" really mean? After all, it is evident that the system is frail, broken and far from perfect. Despite its imperfections, I am also aware that living in a democracy is special. I am lucky. Grateful. How can I ensure that our democracy not only thrives, but improves? Walks its talk. What if we find ourselves suddenly living under a dictatorship? What would I do then? Do I still have what it takes to bring the spirit of peace and loving consciousness to the world - no matter what happens?*

When I returned home, I turned to my "Journal of Inner Inquiry." Writing offers me the opportunity to take an intimate look at my beliefs and values. It helps me discern the core of who I am, the contributions I am determined to make, and the kind of world I yearn to leave behind.

Journal Entry: *As incomprehensible as it may seem, there are days when I wonder if we will always have the honor of living in a democracy. I took it for granted. I don't anymore. I couldn't bear living under a dictatorship. That said, we can only control what we can control, and the rest is noise, chaos, a test of fortitude, courage, resilience and faith. I will continue* *to live with the values that uplift the world. Most of all, I will do everything I can to keep the sacredness of our democracy alive. I am making an internal promise to live the essence of peace, love and hope - no matter what.*

A "Look Within" Experiential Activity

"The more you know yourself,
the more you forgive yourself."

– Confucius

When you have the time and desire, use the following questions to discover new layers of your thoughts and feelings. Join me in my quest towards self-understanding, healing, transformation, clarity, self-discovery and inner peace. Begin your own "Journal of Inner Inquiry."

- *What are my basic values?*

  _____

  _____

  _____

- *Are all parts of my life aligned with my core values?*

  _____

  _____

  _____

- *Am I growing, learning and changing for the better?*

_____

_____

_____

- *What is my personal mission statement?*

_____

_____

_____

- *What dreams do I have for myself? My family? My friends? The world?*

_____

_____

_____

- *What can I do to make the world a more inclusive place in which to live?*

_____

_____

_____

- *What are my unique gifts?*

_____

_____

_____

- *Which issues stir the passion of my soul?*

_____

_____

_____

- *What steps can I take to make a positive difference in the world?*

_____

_____

_____

- *What matters to me?*

_____

_____

_____

- *How can I be the peace I want in the world?*

_____

_____

_____

- *Who are my inspirational mentors and role models?*

_____

_____

_____

- *What qualities do they have in common?*

_____

_____

_____

- *In every situation, am I walking the path of love?*

_____

_____

_____

What Do You Believe?

"If we have no peace, it is because we have forgotten
that we belong to each other."

– Mother Teresa

As I write this chapter, it is October 2020. Earmarks of this
date are a global pandemic, polarization, racial injustice, an
upcoming presidential election, and a democracy that is shaken
to the core. The intensity of this time has been overwhelming
to the soul, and to add to the stress, no unified action plan
has been established to combat the novel coronavirus. Some
people vehemently oppose the idea of wearing a face mask
and refuse to recognize that the coronavirus is real at all.
Others believe that wearing a face mask keeps the virus from
spreading. They are willing to do whatever it takes to care
about the collective whole.

For many, this is also a time for personal reflection, inner inquiry
and awakening. With each new challenge, we find ourselves
asking an infinite number of soul-searching questions.

Please join me in the "Look Within" process as I ask ...

*What are my personal beliefs when I think about democracy,
peace, diversity, immigration, activism, systemic racism, the
Black Lives Matter movement, white privilege, Nationalism,
Globalism, Native American justice, global warming, animal*

rights, religion, spirituality, agnosticism, white supremacy, The Constitution of the United States, The United States Congress, The United States Supreme Court, abortion, the right to choose, suicide, addiction, abuse, mental health, counseling, war, PTSD, veterans, the right to bear arms, LGBTQ rights, poverty, wealth, homelessness, hunger, sex trafficking, human rights, voter suppression, gender equality, altruism, changemaking, possibility, collective consciousness, integrity, truth, hope, justice, empathy, compassion, kindness, generosity, gratefulness, forgiveness, inclusion and love?

- *As I see each of these words, what are my thoughts and feelings?*

_____

_____

_____

- *Am I open to changing my mind?*

_____

_____

_____

- *Am I open to changing my heart?*

_____

_____

_____

- *Do I believe that even the most hardened criminals could one day shift their hearts toward peace and love?*

_____

_____

_____

- *No matter what happens in the world, do I have the strength and faith to continue to believe that peace is possible?*

_____

_____

_____

- *Do I judge those who think and act differently than me?*

_____

_____

_____

- *Am I always empathic and compassionate?*

_____

_____

_____

- *Do I have biases?*

_____

_____

_____

- *Do I discriminate?*

_____

_____

_____

- *Am I prejudiced?*

_____

_____

_____

- *How can I support the world in becoming a more peaceful, kind and loving place?*

_____

_____

_____

- *Am I willing to listen to opinions that differ from my own?*

_____

_____

_____

- *Am I willing to do my best to find common ground?*

_____

_____

_____

As you travel on your soul-searching journey of inner questioning, continue to envision the positive energy of love. Stand tall in your integrity, strength and courage and use the transformational tools in *Peace Dreamer* to keep your flame of hope burning brightly.

In every moment, stand for love,
be love and shine love.

CHAPTER TWO

Inner Peace, Healing, Loving and Living - Part I

"Of My Life"

Be gone you timid heart!

Wonderful

Needs

Another kind

Of strength.

Let the trumpet play courage songs

That I may march

Head high.

– Dr. Geraldine Schwartz

Journeys of Second Adulthood

Ebb and Flow

"Change is the only constant in life."

– Heraclitus

Heraclitus was right when he said, "change is the only constant in life." Some changes feel like a massage to our spirit. If we successfully land a satisfying job, hit the lottery, buy a first home, meet the love of our life, reconcile differences, reunite with a loved one, recover from a serious illness, or welcome a new baby to the world, we glow with optimism and joy. Other changes turn our world as we have known it upside-down. If we experience the death of a loved one, rape, murder, a global pandemic, war, a divorce, imprisonment, a serious illness, unexpected surgery, abuse, addiction, losing a home, unemployment, poverty, hunger or a natural disaster, we are shaken to the core at a time when we need to be stronger than ever.

For both bad times and good, there are a variety of user-friendly strategies and life-changing tools that can ground, strengthen and calm your spirit from inside-out. Each gentle approach will lead you to a place of inner peace and give you the strength you need to accomplish all the dreams that live in your heart.

Transformational Tools for Inner Peace, Healing, Loving and Living

The space between each breath. When life feels out of control, or even when it is running smoothly, invite this transformational tool into your life as often as possible. Stop the world, place your feet firmly on the ground, uncross your arms, return to the present moment, put your hand on your heart, and simply breathe. Feel your entire being in each breath and notice the subtle space between the next inhale and the next exhale. Between each space, consciously relax your body a little more. Unclench your jaw and teeth, relax your neck and shoulders, unfurl your eyebrows, release negative thoughts, and continue to breathe long, slow and deep breaths. Do this exercise as long as it takes to feel better.

Breathe for yourself and breathe for the healing of all humanity.

Self-care during a crisis. When you are called upon to care for someone who is seriously ill, remember to find a way to care for yourself, too. It isn't easy, but it is possible. Adopt the "close your eyes, stop the world, place your hand on your heart, and simply breathe" method, nourish your body by consciously eating healthier meals, drinking more water, taking short naps, visualizing a positive outcome, and breathing in slow sensory walks in nature. Cherish its beauty and allow it to heal your tired spirit. Nature is an outward expression of your inner heart. As Eden, my wise and beautiful sister says, "Nature is the only thing that makes sense."

Do whatever it takes to live in both worlds. Do your best to be a loving caretaker and do your best to take care of yourself, too. Keep believing that life will get better. Hopelessness is the worst disease of all. Don't let it invade your body, mind or spirit. Keep faith and continue to breathe in the positive qualities of resilience, strength and trust.

The healing power of words and thoughts. When my husband suffered a heart attack, we designed a positive affirmation together.

I have the strength and the will to get through this.

We said it aloud, wrote it on post-it notes, imprinted it in our minds, and added the healing tool of visualization to imagine a positive recovery. During COVID-19, we turned to this affirmation again.

> *Power words convey to our subconscious and conscious mind that we can get through anything and everything.*

The healing vibrations of "thought transference." Merriam-Webster dictionary defines thought transference as "the transference of thought from one mind to another." Collins Dictionary adds that it is an "extrasensory means from the mind of one individual to another. Telepathy. The communication between people of thoughts, feelings, desires, involving mechanisms that cannot be understood in terms of known scientific laws, also called thought transference."

Without getting too "woo woo" and out there on another planet about this concept, I am a grounded advocate for the healing tool of "thought transference." When we activate the power of the mind and heart, vibrations of healing, strength and love are sent telepathically to those in emotional, mental, physical or spiritual stress.

Life Wisdom: When I know that someone in my life needs meditative prayer and attention, I place that person in my mind and heart, stand in front of my crystal chakra singing bowls, pick up the mallets, ring each bowl, and allow the sounds to carry beyond the physical form of my room. As the healing sounds continue to vibrate, I visualize the person's face, meditate on their name, picture their healing, send positive thoughts, sing meditative power words, and feel at peace knowing that I am transferring an energy field of love, caring, healing and light that transcends physical distance.

Combining the vibrations of thought transference with the healing power of words. I also add positive affirmations to the thought transference process. When a family member or a friend is suddenly challenged by a "test of fortitude," I place their essence in my mind and heart, ring my crystal chakra bowls, and say ...

> *"May you have the will and the strength to get through this. I am with you and surround you with my love, healing and light."*

When the entire world suffers together from a crisis like COVID-19, I offer a prayer of collective healing ...

> *"May the world have the faith, will and strength to get through this. May we surround each other with love, healing and light."*

Metta Meditation. These heartfelt meditations are patterned after a simple prayer Buddha taught us over 2600 years ago. It is called "The Metta Meditation Prayer of Loving-Kindness." This the prayer I say every morning and every evening ...

"The Metta Meditation Prayer of Loving-Kindness"

May *I* be happy. May *I* be well. May *I* be safe. May *I* be peaceful and at ease.

May *you* be happy. May *you* be well. May *you* be safe. May *you* be peaceful and at ease.

May *we* be happy. May *we* be well. May *we* be safe. May *we* be peaceful and at ease.

I'm Still Here. After a crisis ends, do you ever take the time to acknowledge all the strength and sheer will it took to get through it? As Christopher Robin from *Winnie-the-Pooh* says, "You are braver than you believe and stronger than you think." I have a feeling Christopher Robin describes your determination, resilience, faith and courage perfectly. Stand proudly in this truth. Despite all the challenges, you are still here! Isn't it amazing? I think it is.

There is much more depth to each of us than what we project on the surface. I'm not sure why we tend to keep our troubles private and only show the superficial side of what it means to be human. What if we chose to be more vulnerable and real with each other? What if we took the time to listen to each other? What are your personal experiences of challenge and triumph? Share them all. Inspire people. They will marvel at your resilience with wonder and rejoice at the way your spirit transcended darkness.

Let people know that it is possible to transcend impossible odds!

Underneath the silence. After making music with Alzheimer's patients, I realized on a new level that underneath the silence were beautiful people who have had amazing lives. I also realized that many of us are silent even without any symptoms of Alzheimer's disease. We often hide our history of heartbreaking challenges. We even hide our triumphs. As I thought about this idea more in depth, a new song came through me. The lyrics are applicable to anyone who needs to be remembered, heard, seen, loved and valued. I would say that's everyone, wouldn't you?

I'm Still Here

From the album, *Listen to the Whispers*

I'm still here
I'm still here
I'm still here
No matter what.

I am more than who you see
More than meets the eye
More than who I seem
No matter what.

I'm still here
I'm still here

I'm still here
No matter what.

Please see the light inside me
Know the light inside me
Sense the light inside me
No matter what.

I'm still here
I'm still here
I'm still here
No matter what.

Please take the time to know me
Take the time to see me
Take the time to love me
No matter what.

I'm still here
I'm still here
I'm still here
No matter what

I am love
I am breath
I'm still here
No matter what.

Inner Peace and Happiness

"Peace comes from within. Do not seek it without."

— Siddhārtha Gautama

If I wasn't sick, THEN I'd be happy. If I didn't have to work, THEN I'd be happy. If I could land a job, THEN I'd be happy. If I could find the right partner, THEN I'd be happy. If I could get some peace and quiet around here, THEN I'd be happy. If I could be rich and famous, THEN I'd be happy. If I could have a simpler life, THEN I'd be happy.

Sound familiar? While many of these "if only" chants sound like a key to living a great life, they really don't bring us any closer to happiness at all. True happiness comes from a place deep inside us and has nothing to do with wealth, fame, or what society often defines as "success."

Transformational Tools for Inner Peace, Healing, Loving and Living

Self-Love. How long has it been since you gave yourself adequate acknowledgment, kindness, love and compassion? As cliché as it may sound, how about giving yourself a great big hug of self-acknowledgment right now? Go ahead. No one's looking. Acknowledge how hard you try to be a good person. Wrap your arms around your body and give yourself a megadose of kindness, love and compassion. You don't need to do anything to prove yourself to anyone.

> *You are enough just for being, breathing, and trying to do better than yesterday. Acknowledge yourself and say, "I am enough."*

The stop sign technique. When negative thoughts pop in my mind, I use a technique that keeps my inner critic at bay. I access my imagination, and lo and behold, I see a big red stop sign with a picture of my alter ego painted on its surface. My alter ego notices my behavior, swoops down, picks up the sign, waves it wildly in front my face, and reminds me that I am overdue for an attitude adjustment. "Hey, my friend, stop thinking like that. It's unhealthy. Give yourself a megadose of love and shift your negative thoughts to a higher frequency."

She then provides an entire menu of positive action steps ...

- Choose music that shifts your mood and heals your body, mind and spirit.

- Dance. Move your energy. Make up steps. As part of your freedom dance, move your eyes, eyebrows, fingers, hands, arms, shoulders, neck, head, back, hips, legs, feet, toes - everything.

- Sing out of tune or sing in tune. There are no wrong notes. Only vibrations.

- Hum. Winnie-the- Pooh thinks it's healthy.

- Try to whistle "Somewhere Over the Rainbow."

- Meditate. Give yourself the gift of inner spaciousness. Enjoy the silence.

- Dream big dreams. Dream small dreams. Whatever you do, make time to dream.

- Talk to the birds. Sing to the birds. They can hear you.

- Reduce how long and how often you listen to the news. It can be toxic to your health and addicting to your mind. Watch the news, but in moderation.

- Create. There are latent gifts inside you that are just waiting to come out.

- Take healing walks in nature. There's nothing in the world like it.

- Converse with uplifting people.

- Involve yourself in projects that can make a difference in the world.

- Smile. Giggle. Chuckle. Belly laugh.

- Play a musical instrument. It will balance your left and right brain, fire up your neurons, and the healing sounds of pure vibration will massage your body from inside-out.

- Rediscover how to play and be silly.

- Look up at the unlimited expanse of the sky.

- Knit. Sew. Quilt. Crochet. Each activity is meditative, creative and serves as a positive distraction.

- Plant a garden. There's nothing like getting close to the earth.

- If you live with a dog or a cat, give your furry delight a little extra love.

- Hug a tree. Breathe in its strength, comfort, grounding and majesty.

- Splurge. Buy yourself flowers. You deserve it.

- Sing to your house plants. They hear you.

- Help someone. It's a great way to forget your own troubles.

- Volunteer your time and energy for important causes.

- Wake up early and watch the magical process of the sun rising.

- Make it a point to watch a sunset. Stay for the afterglow, too.

- Follow a rainbow wherever it leads.

- Doodle. Paint. Draw. Sketch. Write. Cook. Bake. Experiment. Invent.

- Watch inspirational movies. Read inspirational books.

- Sign up for a class that is out of your comfort zone. Try something new.

The past is the past: In contrast to what many people believe, there is no shame in making mistakes. We are all perfectly imperfect and it's human to make them. Despite what happened in your past, embrace every inch of your colorful history. Everything that you have gone through has been a lesson in "Life 101." Each lesson was a path that led you to grow into the beautiful person you are today. Do you ever make the same mistakes more than once? I do. Look on the bright side. Repetition creates a deeper opportunity for greater mindfulness and inner healing. Use all your life lessons to forgive yourself, forgive others, and to help make the world a softer place. Step into your life with love in your heart. It is never too late.

> *What happened in the past is what happened in the past. You have the power to define who you are now. Every moment is a new beginning. Make it count.*

Send EVERY person on the planet your love, light and healing - even when it's a challenge. It is easy to support the people we love. It is also easy to support like-minded people who belong to the "same choir." It is much more difficult to offer our spiritual support to those who aren't our "cup of tea." Although it is much more difficult to send love, light and healing to those who have chosen violence, discrimination, bullying, fear and hatred as a way of life, it is important to remember that every human being from every walk of life needs an aura of love, light and healing. You never know. They may sense your "Metta Meditation Prayer of Loving-Kindness" through "thought transference" and be changed by it.

> *If we make a choice to embody the spirit of loving consciousness, we will be able to shift our hearts from fear to love and honor the most authentic definition of "peace begins with me." The only way we can surround the planet with an inclusive vibration of peace is if we surround the planet with an inclusive vibration of love.*

The positive energy of optimism. When you are overloaded with negative thoughts, balance them with a megadose of optimism. "I can do this!" Words matter. "If only I were smarter, richer and more successful" can be replaced with "I define who I am and what is important to me."

If you want to change your life, change your words.

Words have vibrational power. They can hurt, or they can heal. They can give you a sense of optimism, or they can create despair. They can offset the unhelpful voices you hear in your mind, or they can feed your inner critic. It is important to be mindful of the words we say and think. It can make a world of difference.

Power words shift the trajectory of our lives.

When you create positive affirmations, make sure all your sentences and phrases are written in the present tense. Write them as if they are true right now. Before you know it, all your visions and intentions will become more of who you are every day.

Positive Affirmations

- I greet my life with unwavering strength, determination and courage.

- I can, I will, I am.

- I am valuable.

- I share my truth with clarity, strength and love.

- I am my breath. I am love. I am enough. I am.

- I am a beacon of light and hope.

- I am confident.

- I am open to life's unlimited possibilities.

- I claim my full space in the world.

- I stand proudly in who I am.

- I move gracefully with the ebb and flow of change.

- I am a warrior for peace and love.

- I am grateful for all the big and small miracles of life.

- I am my own champion.

- I am my best friend.

- I listen to the voice of my highest intuition.

- I show up for myself.

- I stay in the present.

- All good flows my way.

The "magic wand of golden light" technique. The next concept requires your unbridled imagination. If you have forgotten how to imagine the impossible, invite your inner child to help you ...

Look. Do you see it? It's over there waiting for you. Sparkling. Glowing. Beaming. Luminous. It's a magic wand of golden light, and you and only you can see it. From now on, this enchanted scepter is part of your inner persona and it will be with you wherever you go and whenever you need. When you put it in your hands, you will find that it is supercharged with vibrations of positivity, optimism, happiness, joy, love, protection, wellness, healing and hope. Because you have been chosen as the recipient of this golden treasure, there will be no such thing as a completely miserable day in your life anymore. And the best part? The power of your generous heart and vivid imagination can swirl the vibrations of your magic wand around others, too. Without knowing why, an increase of love, optimism, joy, light and hope will fill their lives. What a gift!

Let's use its magic powers right away. How are you feeling? Are you tired? Grouchy? Angry? Full of fear? Sad? Hurt? Anxious? How would you prefer to feel? You have a choice, you know. You can grumble, stew, withdraw and frown, or you can decide that it's time to make a small shift. If you would like to make a positive shift, close your eyes, take long, slow and deep breaths, put your hand on your heart, and allow yourself to simply be, feel and breathe. In the stillness, imagine a better picture for your life and linger there for awhile. Then, ask the universe to invite qualities into your life that will make this day easier.

Do you need an extra boost of healing? Strength? Patience? Courage? Support? Once you have the qualities you desire visualized in your mind's eye, create positive power words that will support your new attitude. As you say your power words, pick up your magic wand of golden light and swirl it around your body. Let its magical vibrations shift your energy to inner peace, light and hope.

Do you feel a little better now? Is optimism in the air again? If you would like to turn to this magical tool again, you will only need three things. Your magic wand of golden light, a keen imagination, and trust in the ebb and flow of life.

Congratulations! You are now one of the world's official lightworkers and an energy force for unlimited possibility and joy. It is up to the lightworkers of the world to create positive changes and embody strong vibrations of peace, healing, hope and love. Is your magic wand of golden light with you now? I hope so. Don't forget it.

Be your own magic genie!

Journal writing: Let all your feelings flow from your mind and heart and onto the pages of a special notebook or journal. Don't worry about spelling, punctuation and grammar. Just allow anything that is stored inside you to flow out in a steady stream of consciousness. Write down the dreams you have for yourself, decide on your definition of happiness, inner peace and success, and imagine what dreams you envision for our world.

Write down all your worries, anger, hopes, confusions, and unanswered questions, too. Journal writing releases all the "icky stuff." All the toxicity. All the thoughts that clog your mind, spirit, soul and heart. Can you imagine how free you will feel if you let them go? Just let it rip.

Free yourself to be yourself.

What are your forgotten dreams? Have you lost the energy to dream bigger dreams for yourself and to dream bigger dreams for the world? I think it's time for a big change, don't you? Invite all your forgotten starry-eyed dreams to *"Life 101."* Exercise this muscle and encourage your inner child to dream along with you. Has your life gotten too serious? If so, there are all kinds of imaginative ways to bring out the essence of your inner child. You can dance to your heart's delight in the privacy of your bedroom, sing loud and proud out of tune or in tune, play a kazoo, fly a kite, blow bubbles, scribble, finger paint, climb a tree, (or imagine it in your mind's eye), and allow all your deepest wishes to soar towards the stars and beyond. When you were young, what were your interests? What did you like to do for fun? Are there any hints from the good parts of your childhood that you could transfer into your life now? Make a list of all your innate abilities, strengths and positive personality traits and use them as the compass to your life.

Albert Einstein: When I was a child, I would look out the window at school and daydream. It got me into trouble with a teacher or two, but it didn't stop me. It was just in my nature to daydream. After all, even Albert Einstein said, "imagination is more important than knowledge." Daydreaming led me to truths that still stir in my heart to this day. I had dreams of singing, composing and performing on stage, and it has been one of my career paths in life. I had dreams of writing books, and I have written them. I had dreams of discovering like-minded people to help me build a world of peace and love, and I have found them. Even if you prefer to be practical and realistic, entertain the idea of daydreaming at least ten minutes a day. When a new idea, goal, vision or dream pops into your head, write it down. What action steps can you take? What else can you do to discover the gifts and the goodness of who you are? Trust that the universe is constantly working with you in a timing that is filled with grace and love.

Daydream!

Under the surface: If you think that your life is standing still and you're going nowhere fast, I know that the opposite is true. Under the surface of stillness, there is constant humming of personal growth and transformation. You never know when there will be a delightful surprise. At any moment, there could be an exciting opportunity to live a new purpose. It's worth hanging around to find out what's next, because as tough as life can become at times, it can also shift towards light and joy in a New York minute.

Trust.

Attention all dreamers: What does your heart want? What are the whispers of your inner voice saying to you? What is your innermost truth? Honor your dreams and embrace the fairy dust that lights your way. Shift your mindset to self-belief and unlimited possibilities. When you believe in yourself, anything and everything is possible. Keep that fire in your belly. Always maintain hope for yourself and for the world. Remember who you are deep down in your soul, and if someone you know forgets who *they* are, embody what the writer, Arne Gorborg, eloquently communicated years ago ...

> *"To love someone is to learn the song in their heart and sing it to them when they have forgotten it."*

Listen to the Whispers

"Be a peacemaker in everyday life. Display peace in everything you do. Be peace. Live in peace."

– Buddhist Proverb

Here we are. Another day. How will you choose to live it? What thoughts will swirl in your mind? What feelings will bubble up? What words will you say? Will you honor the dreams in your heart? How can you bring more peace into your life and into the lives of others? How can you offer more kindness and compassion to the world? How can you honor and respect more of your true essence? How can you honor and respect those who are different from you?

Allow sacred moments for simply being, breathing, and opening your heart to love. With your heart open, ask the universe a question that has been on your mind for awhile. Are you feeling confused? Stressed? Angry? Sad? Frustrated? Do you wonder if there will ever be peace in our world? In your family? In yourself?

Ask a higher consciousness from within to guide you.

Intimate answers may come in the form of a strong inner voice, a quiet whisper, or an unexpected "sign." A sign could be as simple as a songbird that decides to flutter in front of your eyes. Who knows? The songbird may be a departed loved one who came to visit you for a reason. Ask your loved one a question that lives in the deepest part of your heart. Then, listen.

To hear the voice of your highest wisdom and intuition, imagine an energy center in the middle of your forehead called the "third eye." This energy center is an inner vortex that invites your deepest wisdom and highest intuition to open. Invite your third eye to expand, and as its vibration becomes stronger, shout a resounding *YES* to life!

- Say YES to courage.

- Say YES to strength.

- Say YES to persistence.

- Say YES to resilience.

- Say YES to determination.

- Say YES to healing.

- Say YES to forgiveness.

- Say YES to empathy.

- Say YES to compassion.

- Say YES to big dreams.

- Say YES to small dreams.

- Say YES to all your innate gifts and talents.

- Say YES to new beginnings.

- Say YES to exciting opportunities.

- Say YES to trust.

- Say YES to faith.

- Say YES to self-belief.

- Say YES to self-care.

- Say YES to diversity celebration.

- Say YES to a world of kindness.

- Say YES to life's unlimited joys.

- Say YES to inner peace.

- Say YES to peace on our earth.

- Say YES to love.

- Say YES to hope.

Shifting the Lens of Life

"The soul should always stand ajar, ready to welcome
the ecstatic experience."

– Emily Dickinson

Good morning! Good afternoon!
Good evening! Good day!

Adjusting the lens. I love the phrases, "good morning," "good afternoon," "good evening" and "good day." When someone says "good morning" to me, it feels good. Unfortunately, I'm not sure everyone likes these phrases as enthusiastically as I do. It depends. If I say a chipper "good morning" to a neighbor, they might smile and say "good morning" back, or they might respond with "What's *good* about it?"

How we react to even a "good morning" often depends on
the lens in which we are viewing the ups
and downs of life.

I will always say "good morning." I know first-hand that a simple "good morning" could be the attention and visibility someone needs. It might snap them out of a grouchy mood, put a smile on their face, and shift their attitude. You never know.

A small risk, a simple act of kindness, and a new lens.
Imagine!

A beautiful park, two different people with two different attitudes, and their dogs. The "adjusting the lens of life" idea reminds me of a story my husband told me the other day. He was fishing at a state park. On his left, he heard a man swear at his dogs with words that I can't share in a book on peace and love. He went on and on, ranting and raving. On his right, he heard a woman talk to her dogs in the kindest and most loving tones imaginable. "Oh, sweetie. Good job. Way to go. I love you so much."

Each person had different perceptions, emotions, thoughts and moods. The woman felt happy. The man was in a foul mood. If he could have shifted his attitude, his day would have been so much better. After all, he was surrounded by the beauty of calm water, beautiful pine trees, open space, and the healing power of nature. Sadly, none of it mattered. His heart was too closed to notice anything that could heal him. In contrast, the woman adored her dogs and her surroundings. Her heart was open, her attitude was positive, and her lens was adjusted toward happiness, joy, contentment and love. Two different people in the same state park, each one with a different attitude and a different lens.

Kindness arguments. I have another lens-shifting story. My granddaughter, Maya, age 7, came up with it. She said that there is such a thing as a "kindness argument." Because I am fascinated by two polarized words that wind up having a good outcome, I asked her to tell me more about her concept.

She said, "It's when someone says, "You go first," and the other person says, "No, you go first." They go back and forth for awhile until someone agrees to go first. They had a "kindness argument." They thought more about the other person than themselves."

I asked her for more examples. Maya said, "Okay. Two people are driving on the highway. One person wants to cut in front of the other car and the other person doesn't want that to happen. One of them changes their mind and signals with their hand, "Okay, you go first." The other person signals with their hand, "No, you go first." Finally, one person agrees to go first and waves a friendly "thank you" to the other driver. They had a "kindness argument."

"One more example, Grelody. What if my three-year-old sister, Eva, wants to play with my toy and I want to play with it, too? I might say, "No, I want it." She might say a little louder, "No, I want it." I might say even louder, "No, I want it." Then, I stop, think, shift my heart, and let her use it.

"That's a kindness argument, Grelody. When things happen like that, it brings good into the world."

I just loved my deep discussion with Maya. Children can be so much wiser than grown-ups. I also loved the way she understood the concept of shifting our hearts and compromising for the greater good of the collective whole.

Humanity 101. A new kind of list. We are always writing to-do lists with endless tasks and activities. What if we took the time to create a new kind of list? A Humanity 101 list? This list taps into our core values and the softer and more meaningful side of life. As you begin to think about this concept, here are a few ideas from my book, *Heart-Dreamer: Stepping into Life, Love, Creativity and Dreams - No Matter What* ...

Love. Remember that all paths lead to love.

Reach out. Be a beacon of light, inspiration and hope.

Give. Give without any expectations.

Good vibes. Aim for optimism. Wherever you go, spread the power of love.

Feel. Keep your heart open.

Backbone. Stand in your truth. Speak up. Give yourself an empowered voice.

Help. Do whatever you can to make this world a better place.

People. Listen, uplift and inspire.

Forgive. Open your heart to forgiveness.

Awaken. Stay awake, aware, conscious and fully present.

Open. Learn from people who are different from you.

Imagine. See your life as you would like it to be. See the world as you would like it to be. Believe!

Dream. No matter what is happening, visualize a world of mutual understanding and peaceful conflict-resolution. What does it look like? Sound like? Breathe hope into every one of your cells and never give up on your vision for a more inclusive and peaceful world. Keep your eyes up on the horizon and continue to dream of a humanity that embodies unity, kindness and peace.

Do your best to work through difficult issues with family, friends, and a world that challenges your faith in humanity. Always remind yourself of all the *good* that exists inside you. Always remind yourself of all the *good* that exists in the world.

I end these thoughts with a warm *good* morning, *good* afternoon, *good* evening and *good* day to you. Keep your lens adjusted towards all the *good* that life has to offer, and when you have an argument, do what Maya suggests. Think about shifting it into a "kindness argument."

Enjoy the following affirmations of "loving-kindness." Write them down on post-it notes, say them, think them, sing them, memorize them, and imagine that every word is already true.

May I have a good day and may all good flow my way. May you have a good day and may all good flow your way. May everyone on the planet have a good day and may all good flow their way.

How to Protect Yourself From Negative Energy

"Stay away from negative people. They have a
problem for every solution."

– Albert Einstein

Do you get a little defensive when someone wants to confront
you about something you did or said that offended them? I do.
But not for long. You see, I have a secret strategy that keeps
me safe from absorbing negative energy. In fact, my strategy
has magic powers.

Before I share my pearls of wisdom with you, remember that
you have a choice. You have the power to decide whether to
engage with them or not. If their zealousness for confrontation
is a familiar pattern, and if you are sure that your time with
them will bring you down and destroy your spirit, advocate for
yourself. As respectfully as possible, say "No." You can choose
to explain further or just leave it at that.

You can make another choice, too. If you would like to have
the discussion but need extra time to gather your strength and
courage, arrange for another day that would work better for
you and your needs.

Of course, there is one more choice. If you are up to it, hold your
head high, straighten your posture, stand in your backbone,

open your heart, and hear them out right then and there. Is it at all possible that there could be an element of truth in what they are about to convey? Are you curious? Hopeful?

What if the confrontation leads to a good outcome?

If you choose to engage with this person, remember to breathe. Breathe in *your* breath, not theirs, and stay as centered and grounded as possible. Stand tall, uncross your legs, unfold your arms, and place both feet confidently on the ground. Most of all, don't take their words and actions personally.

> *When someone is upset, there are often deep wounds that stir inside their soul that have nothing at all to do with you.*

A magical remedy. While it is tempting to go down the dark rabbit hole with them, choose a higher path. When someone clashes against my soft empathic nature, I use the power of creative visualization to reach for my imaginary golden zipper. It's not an ordinary zipper, of course. It vibrates superpowers of love, safety and protection. It also keeps me safe from absorbing any toxic energy that might be coming my way.

During a confrontation, (and before, if possible), access your imagination, too. See yourself holding a golden zipper and use its superpowers to zip yourself up from the bottoms of your feet to the top of your head, down your back, and then return to your feet again.

You are now surrounded with an auric field of safety, protection, strength, courage, trust, and inner healing.

Life Wisdom: Your magic zipper is a protective energy field that can change its color, thickness, dimension, length, and shape at your request. You and only you are in control of its powers. It will do anything and everything to protect you from harm. It not only prevents the absorption of negative energy, but it can do even more than that. It can shift your heart from fear to love, and it can help you picture the possibility of giving birth to a healthier relationship. One of understanding, compassion, empathy, forgiveness, love and peace. It could happen. You never know.

CHAPTER THREE

True Stories of Love, Healing, Transformation and Peace

"Be yourself. Not your idea of what you think somebody else's idea of yourself should be."

– Henry David Thoreau

The Worst Best Thing That Ever Happened

"No one heals himself by wounding another."

— St. Ambrose

Once upon a time there was a child who was constantly bullied and teased. She never understood why she was the target of physical and emotional abuse, but she was. Was the bullying based on religious prejudice? Was it because she was too shy, too poor, too tall, too short, too smart, not smart enough, didn't wear the "in" clothes?

Maybe she was just an easy target. She was silent. Equally as sad, the kids who witnessed the bullying were silent, too. Now that this child is an adult, she thinks back to those days ...

If only I hadn't been silent. If only the kids who witnessed the abuse hadn't been silent, either.

Life Wisdom: As her mind flashed back to this difficult time, she realized how strong she had been, too. Despite the abuse, she never lost faith that people were better than this. They just needed to awaken their soul to a higher consciousness of love, acceptance, tolerance and peace. They needed to realize on a deeper level that all hearts beat in the same way and that feelings are the same for everyone.

"Keep faith in the goodness of people," the wisdom whisper said. "Don't lose hope. Set an example. Be a role model. Find a way to show the world how to be love, shine love and stand for love. When you grow up, choose work that will make a difference in the consciousness of others."

The prejudice she experienced as a child motivated her to find a way to open hearts, raise awareness, and create an inclusive and loving world. As a result, she became a "you can change your life" writer, singer, "peace through music" composer, performing artist, recording artist, sound healer, motivational speaker and educator. She made sure that each word in every book, song, workshop, presentation and lesson contained messages of love, inclusion, healing and peace.

One more thing. The child in the story is me, and I am asking everyone who reads this book to take a stand on behalf of diversity celebration, respect and love. If you see or hear a destructive situation that doesn't feel right in your soul, give yourself a strong voice. Don't be complicit in your silence.

Please work with me to help make our one precious world a more inclusive and heart-centered place.
Thank you.

From Heartbreak to Healing

"How wonderful it is that nobody need wait a single
moment before starting to improve the world."

– Anne Frank

Oklahoma City, April 19, 1995. The Alfred P. Murrah Federal
Building had just been bombed by two domestic terrorists. Eight
hundred people were injured. One hundred and sixty-eight
people died. Some were children.

When I heard about it, I had an ache in my heart to help
anyway I could. I thought about it day and night. Out of the
blue, I received a call from Dr. Norma J. Leslie, a heart-centered
professor from the University of Oklahoma. She was familiar
with many of the songs on my albums, and because she knew
about my positive lyrics and the essence of my heart, she asked
if I would be willing to travel there to perform a concert of hope
and healing. Initially, I was concerned that I might not have
enough experience to meet her request, but in the next breath,
I realized that I had just been asked to step into my highest
purpose.

***I shifted my heart to a determined YES and
stepped into my new mission with faith,
courage and trust.***

On the day of the concert, I felt a strong need to visit the site of
the bombing. Dr. Leslie's son, Brad, drove me there, and as we

looked at all the teddy bears and hand-written notes, I sobbed. Grief, anger and heartbreak permeated the air, and because my own heart was breaking, I silently questioned if I had enough strength inside me to perform at all.

Then, out of nowhere, I spotted a small tree standing tall in the middle of all the destruction. Miraculously, it survived the bombing. I dubbed it "the tree of hope." As we drove to the University of Oklahoma to get ready for the concert, I heard a strong inner voice say ...

Your mission is to be a lightworker amid the darkness.

As I walked on the stage, my old enemy, *doubt*, tortured me again. "Don't you realize that there is no quick fix to healing? Your music won't offer solace to anyone."

Suddenly, in the middle of all my doubts, a beautiful butterfly flew on the stage. It landed on my microphone, fluttered all around me, and then flew over to my left shoulder and stayed there for awhile. Intuitively and gratefully, I knew that the butterfly came to inspire the promise of hope and healing.

A sudden rush of confidence surged through me as I stepped forward to sing a song of unity. It was called, "One Planet." *We're all one people, all one nation, all one planet, together we can live ...*

As the audience sang along, I heard the whispers of my inner voice again. "Ask everyone to step off the bleachers. Meet each other. Connect them. Heart to heart. Soul to soul." I hesitated. "Would everyone do it, or would I make a fool out of myself?"

I decided to take a leap of faith and listen to the whispers of my highest intuition. As I continued to sing the "One Planet" song, I was amazed to witness people of all colors, ages and religions step down from the bleachers, walk over to each stranger and introduce themselves, give each other hugs, cry in each other's arms, and share some of their overwhelming grief heart to heart and soul to soul. In one unexpected miraculous moment, I understood why I had been given this honor.

Dr. Leslie must have had an intuitive feeling that I would be able to connect people with people in one community of love.

The highest meaning of the "One Planet" song came to life right before my eyes, and a tragic event that was meant to devastate the community, served to unite it. Just as the butterfly promised, I witnessed the power of healing, unity and hope.

One Planet

From the album, *Celebrate!*

We're all one people
All one nation,
All one planet,
Together we can live.

We're all the colors of one rainbow
All the feelings of one heart
All the music of one voice
Let's reach for a brand-new start.

We're all one people
All one nation,
All one planet,
Together we can live.

Lots of struggles are the same for all of us
Each other's hearts we really do know
We're all connected with each other
Remember that, and don't feel low.

We're all one people
All one nation,
All one planet,
Together we can live.

Show your kindness to each other
Know that we are one
There's magic in caring for another
Your love shines like the sun.

We're all one people
All one nation,
All one planet,
Together we can live.

Sing this song to each other
Dance with joy hand in hand
We're everybody's sister and brother
So, strike up the *One Planet* band!

We're all one people
All one nation,
All one planet,
Together we can live.

PEACE

A Teacher Named Tonia

"There is a candle in your heart ready to be kindled.
There is a voice in your soul ready to be filled. You
feel it, don't you?"

– Rumi

My music class ended. As my students waited in line to leave
for their next class, Tonia asked if she could sing a song. She
added, "It's a long song, Cheryl Melody. It just got released on
the radio and I memorized all the verses. I love it. I know our
class is over, but I promise to make the song shorter. Please?"

As I weighed the pros and cons, my mind hopped all over
the place ...

*What song will she sing? Shouldn't I preview it
to make sure that the lyrics are acceptable? If the
lyrics aren't appropriate, how can I be encouraging to her young spirit and yet set firm boundaries?
What if I don't know the song? As her music teacher,
shouldn't I?*

Despite all my fears and doubts, Tonia's sweet demeaner and
persistence inspired me to let go of my insecurities and offer
her my full presence and attention. As she sang "Firework," by
Katy Perry, I was moved to tears. The lyrics lifted me up at a
time when I needed it most.

"You just gotta ignite the light and let it shine."

Life Wisdom: The lyrics were my healing medicine and Tonia was my personal earth angel who was sent to uplift my spirit. Thank you, sweet child. If I had responded to her request with "no, maybe next time," I would have missed an opportunity for personal growth.

As I drove home, I looked within and asked ...

How can I be less reactive and more flexible in the moment? How can I surrender to the unknown and the unplanned more easily? How can I offer my students more opportunities to show me what is in their hearts, too?

We never know, at any moment, who will be the teacher and who will be the student.

An Alternative to Hard Work

"Whatever you can do or dream, you can begin it.
Boldness has genius, power and magic in it."

– Johann Wolfgang von Goethe

I decided to take a break from one of my intense projects, walked outside, climbed into my colorful hammock, looked up at the clear blue sky, and asked the universe, "Should I feel guilty about taking a break right now? What if I lose my momentum? Isn't resting a form of doing, too?" The universe, (my strong inner voice and highest wisdom), answered, "Renew, refresh and regroup. Breathe. If you watch the clouds go by for awhile, you will be even more productive."

That's all I needed to hear. I released the philosophy of "hard work is the only way" and made a conscious decision to temporarily let go of my project. It wasn't easy. I don't like to take breaks. This time, I listened to the whispers of the universe and resisted the impulse to get off the hammock to return to work. Instead, I stepped into the mystery of timelessness.

Many of us believe that hours of nose-to-the-grindstone hard work is the only way to delve into a project, achieve success, or make our dreams come true. I was brought up with this philosophy, too. While it may seem like a logical way to achieve our goals, there is another ingredient that is equally as important. It may seem counterintuitive, but if we take a breather, give into a short nap, or enjoy a healing walk in nature, we will be rewarded with fresh energy and perspective.

As I looked up at the sky, I remembered all the magical moments in my life when I didn't have to work hard to make my dreams come true. When we open ourselves to the mystical magic of the unknown, many moments of serendipity dance towards us when we least expect it.

You Never Know

"When you begin to notice the coincidences in your life and pay attention to them, they'll open you up to your glory, your greatness and your path forward."

— Barbara Gaughen-Muller

- I was in the middle of recording a new album and had my repertoire written in stone. Suddenly, an original song whooshed through me. I was thrilled.

Celebrate!

From the album, *Celebrate!*

It's a good life, so live it
Live it to the fullest
It's a good life, live it every day.

Every minute, every hour
Every second, every flower
It's a good life, live it every day.

See the birds and the butterflies
All people through loving eyes
And thank your lucky stars above.

Share your joys and your sorrows
Don't fret about tomorrows
And remember to give yourself some love.

It's a good life, so live it
Live it to the fullest
It's a good life, live it every day.

Every minute, every hour
Every second, every flower
It's a good life, live it every day.

And remember to sing your song
There is no right or wrong
Don't matter if you sing out of tune

Free your voice, let it rise
Feels good, you'll be surprised
Can you sing your heart's song soon?

It's a good life, so live it
Live it to the fullest
It's a good life, live it every day

Every minute every hour
Every second every flower
It's a good life, live it every day.

Shortly after the album's release, I received an email. "How can I purchase a song I heard the other day? I loved it." My mind immediately began to hop around with endless chatter ...

I wonder which of my songs gave him such joy? It couldn't be "Celebrate!" No one knows about it. I just released it. Plus, I'm not famous. I'm just an independent artist funding my projects on a shoestring budget, and besides, marketing isn't my strength. Maybe he lives in Massachusetts, too. That's probably how he heard about it. Maybe he knows my recording engineer.

The *real* story amazed me ...

He didn't live in Massachusetts. In fact, he lived in California. As he waited for the traffic light to turn green, he heard a catchy song playing in the car next to his. He loved its upbeat message and yelled to the driver, "What's the name of that song and who is the singer?" She responded, "Celebrate!," and that's Cheryl Melody!"

Serendipity!

-   After I finished performing a "Peace Begins with Me" concert, one of the teachers ran up to the stage with glowing praise and a warm smile and enthusiastically suggested that I immediately contact her friend, Bob Silverstein. She added, "Bob has devoted his life to peace, too. You need to meet each other. I think you would have lots to talk about." I knew that her heartfelt words were wisdom whispers from the universe, and without any hesitation, I called him that day. As we got to know each other by email and shared our mutual dreams for a world of peace, he asked if I would be willing to read a short children's play that he had written with his friend, Steve Diamond. It was entitled, "One Day in Peace."

I loved the play's messages about inclusion, diversity, cooperation, teamwork and effective communication, and as I continued to read the script, original music started to flow through me. The experience was intense and exciting as creative ideas for the play's expansion came to me in the middle of the night. Bob and Steve soon gave me their permission to transform "One Day in Peace" into other formats, and in less than six months, there were new "peace through music" songs, albums, a three-act musical play, adult workshops, musical peace gatherings, and national performances for both children and adults.

You never know what can happen if you open your heart to all the unknown mysteries of life.

- After writing my first book, *Shift of Heart: Paths to Healing and Love*, I wanted to find like-minded people to join me in mirroring all the values shared in this book. As a result, a large *Shift of Heart* Facebook community continues to evolve, one heart-centered person at a time. In this global community, we honor our truth and wisdom, believe in the well-being of the collective whole, and offer each other compassion, kindness and unconditional love. I just needed to take a risk, write a mission statement, and ask if anyone would like to join me. After all, what was the worst that could happen by reaching out? My life would stay the same. Instead, I received an enthusiastic response from people all over the world who wanted to actively participate in my mission to spread love. We gather as heart-dreamers, healers and lightworkers on behalf of our collective dream to create a planet of inclusion, peace and hope.

Take a risk. You never know.

- I was folding laundry, and other than that, I had nothing else in my mind. Suddenly, I saw **HEART-DREAMER** flash through my mind. The font was bold, large and clear, and there was a distinct hyphen symbol between the words, "heart" and "dreamer." The hyphen seemed to be an important reminder that there is a deep connection between the yearnings of the heart and the passions of our dreams. I tried to push this unexpected vision away and dismiss it as insignificant, but something inside me urged me to pay attention. After all, this kind of thing has happened to me before.

I knew that I was just touched by another
wisdom whisper.

From that day on, a new self-help book began to make its way into the world. *Heart-Dreamer: Stepping into Life, Love, Creativity and Dreams - No Matter What* has been floating in the universe encouraging everyone to honor the truth of their dreams in the same way I follow my own.

Trust!

Serendipity and You: Open your heart to the magical mystery of the unplanned and unexpected miracles in life. I'm sure you have countless stories of serendipitous moments, too. I am also sure that there will be many more amazing moments that won't need overplanning and overthinking. Professionally, pushing the river is that old nose-to-the-grindstone philosophy. While I believe in hard work, I also know that balancing my strong work ethic with "beingness" and downtime are winning combinations.

Breathe in skipping-through-the-meadow lightness at all the unexpected surprises and wisdom whispers that are just around the corner.

Stories of Personal Growth, Transformation and Healing

The following stories were written by members of the "Shift of Heart" Facebook community

Laurel - It wasn't easy to find out that I had cancer, but over time, I decided not to crumble. I decided to fight. I am adamant for my healing and I am adamant to survive this. Once I got over the traumatic news, I told myself that I will get through this, and God, my dad and my friends will support me. I changed my vibration to the positive. I know I CAN DO IT and be a survivor!!!

Faith - Years ago, I worked in a software development organization. I was a developer. Laura was a new tester. I found it tiring to work with her, because every time she found an issue, it seemed like she treated it like an emergency. She was hyper about her work and I always felt like she didn't understand protocols, severities, or priorities. I felt frustrated whenever I had to work with her.

Then, I was assigned to a new project and one tester. Laura. I realized that if I wanted to keep my sanity, I was going to need to learn how to work with her without wanting to tear my hair out. I stopped by her office right after the assignment came out. I told her that we were assigned together, and I thought we should get to know each other better. After talking with her for awhile, I realized that she was one of these hyper types where everything in her life was an emergency. She bounced off the walls as a normal part of her day, and she wasn't doing this to drive me crazy. It was just who she was. I shifted how I approached her and how I worked with her.

The project was a success, and we are still best friends thirty years and many jobs later! We email or text each other several times a day. Yes, life is still an emergency for her, and she is still hyper about everything. She's the total opposite of me in that way. But it's just who she is. Recognizing that it is just who she is has adjusted my expectations and preconceptions that she's not trying to make me crazy. She is just doing what she normally does. This new perspective made all the difference in the world.

Autumn - Sometimes, when I keep repeating the same mistakes expecting different results, I wake up just in time to have an AHA moment. I've learned that I need to think of my future when it comes to relationships. What am I going to do when I'm seventy, eighty, ninety? Repeat the same mistakes? I know that it's time for me to wake up, smell the coffee, and make the necessary changes I need to make while I can. I also know that Spirit is waiting to help me if I just ask and if I take positive action.

Alice - When my husband and caregiver died, I saw no way through. Some days I went to bed and pulled the covers over my head, but I was so instinctively drawn to Reiki, healing and moving forward, I could not stop the avalanche of love and wisdom coming to me from friends, teachers, and the universe.

Cynthia - I love sharing my story about an angry lady in my condo who would stalk me just to yell at me. At first, I was angry and fought back. Then, I realized that my reaction was just feeding her, and I searched to find a better way. I realized that I needed to listen to her. Man! That was tough. But as I listened, I discovered that there was one thing in her rant that I literally could fix. I jumped on this idea and took care of fixing something that was broken in her condo. In her next rant, she thanked me. Now every time she rants, I listen for what I can do to help her. Now she always says she loves me after she yells at me! It was amazing that someone this violent taught me how to listen deeply. I never realized how little I listened to people until this situation came into my life. Conflict is a good teacher.

Jean - When I least expected it, I was asked to take over an urgent and critical medical situation on behalf of my ex-husband. After struggling and suffering many years from my husband's addiction, alcoholism and abuse, I found the strength to shift my heart and take care of him - no matter what. After I gave his situation my total energy for a long period of time, my soul's wellspring was completely depleted. Once he was well enough to receive other care, I realized that the right thing to do now was to take care of myself above anyone else. This shift in my perception gave me the strength, the courage, and the belief that I will persevere beyond this hard time, and no matter what, I will remember to put my own oxygen mask on before giving it away. I understood on a new level that I matter just as much as anyone else and that what I gave him was in fact good enough. I'm grateful that I had a shift in my heart that led me to love and acknowledge myself more than ever before.

Thia - No matter how hard I helped my mom raise my half-sister and deal with all her problems, my mom never loved me. When I moved to Arizona seven years ago, my sister, who also lived there, moved my mom to Arizona, too. By taking this action, we could both share in our mom's care. Because I saw my mom more often, I was finally able to heal myself, and to my delight, I was also able to help my mom see the magic in life. Every time a wish we made came true, I told her that it was the magic we had by being together. She loved this idea so much and began to catch life's magic even before I did! It was the happiest I ever saw her, and it was the happiest I felt about our relationship, too!

When I learned to love myself, I could learn to love my mother and she could love me back. I am so grateful that I got this chance. Lately, my sister created a space where my mom and I don't see each other much anymore, but every time she sees me, she lights up. I feel so blessed to have come full circle with my mother. I am very content.

Diane - I've always believed in our connection to Nature and the Universe. Never understood it, but always accepted it. This belief has opened me to incredible experiences that many people would call miracles. I'm not going to argue with that.

Here's just one example. Marriage to my high school sweetheart ended after seven years. I knew I couldn't stay in the same city, because our circle of friends and my business associates were all interconnected with his family. When I announced that I was moving to San Francisco, everyone asked, "Why?" The only answer was that it seems like the right thing to do.

The first thing I did after my furniture arrived in my new San Francisco apartment was to set up my stereo. Music has always been an especially important part of my life. This was in the era of cassette players, long before CDs. The first tape played about twelve minutes, and then I heard a CB conversation between two truck drivers. I switched to the radio and tuned into a classical-music station. No problem. Then, I put a record on the turntable and played it. No problem. There was only one way to hook up the system, so I knew I hadn't done anything wrong.

I decided to find someone to help me resolve the problem with the cassette player. The next day, I opened the phone book to the "stereo" section. The list of stores and repair facilities filled three pages! I started with "A." Everyone I talked with told me that I needed to replace my cassette player, until I got to companies that began with "S." I called *Sound Systems* and talked with a nice gentleman who needed to know what part of San Francisco I lived in. "Glen Park" was my answer. He asked, "Can you see Sutro Tower from your home?"

If you've ever been to San Francisco, Sutro Tower is the humongous red mast-like spire that dominates the western hills. I could see it clearly. "You've got RFI, and I can fix it." I learned later that Radio Frequency Interference was common in San Francisco. I agreed to bring my cassette player to him. He didn't charge me for the parts or the labor.

The evening that he delivered and installed my repaired cassette player, I made dinner for him. It was the least I could do to show my gratitude. A five-year friendship blossomed between us, based on our mutual love of music, and grew into a love that has lasted for 41 years of commitment to each other.

Was it Divine Intervention that inspired me to move to San Francisco when I could have chosen any city in the United States? I believe it was. I also believe that the Universe provides us with miraculous opportunities if we're open to the possibilities.

Do you have a story of personal growth,
transformation and healing, too?
Write it down in a journal and
share it with others.

CHAPTER FOUR

A Wake-Up Call

"No matter what happens in your life,
return to the center of love."

– Cheryl Melody Baskin

What Happened?

"Never be in a hurry; do everything quietly and in a calm spirit. Do not lose your inner peace for anything whatsoever, even if your whole world seems upset."

– St. Francis de Sales

First, the novel coronavirus spread through China, Nepal, France, Australia, Malaysia, Singapore, South Korea, Vietnam, Taiwan, Philippines, Russia, Spain, Sweden, the United Kingdom, Canada, Germany, Japan, Singapore, United Arab Emirates, Italy, Israel, Iran, Kuwait, Bahrain, Iraq, Oman, Norway, Romania, Greece, Georgia, Pakistan, Afghanistan, North Macedonia, Brazil, India, Estonia, Denmark, Northern Ireland, the Netherlands, Wales, Saudi Arabia, Turkey, the Ivory Coast, Bolivia, the Democratic Republic of the Congo ...

Then, it happened. COVID-19 was an equal opportunity disease. It was our turn. "We're all in this together" seemed like an appropriate slogan and many of us were asked to live up to the slogan by staying home until the worst was over.

I was more than willing to do my part. In fact, I had moments when it felt euphoric to be given the formal permission to curl up in my cocoon of safety and not feel guilty about it. I looked forward to snuggling up and relaxing, but a shift in my mindset propelled me into an unexpected burst of creative purpose and energy. I could hear my inner voice saying ...

"Don't withdraw or give into your fears. Come out of hiding, step into your full potential, stay strong, and find positive ways to serve as a beacon of hope to others."

I immersed myself in writing self-help articles, supporting my *Shift of Heart* Facebook community, contributing to The Visioneers International Network roundtable, reading inspirational books, experimenting with new recipes, ringing my crystal healing bowls, singing songs of hope, connecting with my grandchildren on FaceTime, chatting with family and friends, teaching early childhood music classes on Zoom, attending online workshops, performing concerts on YouTube, writing in my journal, and experiencing pure delight as I watched the hummingbirds sip sweet nectar from the feeders.

I wanted to focus on all these good-for-my-spirit projects all day and every day, but I knew that it was equally important to have serious conversations with my husband. We made sure that we were both on the same page when it came to protecting ourselves, each other, and the community. We also solidified our funeral plans "just in case." Discussing death was my least favorite activity, but I did my best to participate in all the to-dos surrounding the "what if we die in the next few months" process.

We also listened to the news much more frequently than before the pandemic, and what we heard was horrifying. COVID-19 cases and deaths were steadily climbing, testing was scarce and imperfect, there was no unified plan, and there was a shocking lack of personal protective equipment for all our first responders, healthcare professionals and essential frontline workers. There were also flaws in the equal distribution of food, hoarding was rampant, and masks, thermometers, toilet paper and disinfecting wipes were scarce.

There is a saying imprinted on my coffee mug. "Peace. It does not mean to be in a place where there is no noise, trouble or hard work. It means to be doing those things and still be calm in your heart." Before COVID-19, I did my best to adhere to this beautiful wisdom. Now, it was difficult.

How can all these inequities exist? How can there be such a lack of caring? Why is there so much chaos?

Despite these thoughts, I balanced my life by focusing on small moments of joy. I delighted in my grandchildren and our talks on FaceTime, the beautiful sky, the gentle breeze, my husband's hug, the warmth of the sun, the gentle rain, and the call of the birds. I enjoyed any activity that fed my spirit, and as ironic as it seemed, life still felt strangely manageable.

Until it wasn't. Nights were the worst. Anxieties and fears swept under the rug during the day caught up to me at night. Finally, I decided that enough was enough. It was time to reach for all the centering approaches that I had used before COVID-19 changed my life.

CHAPTER FIVE

Love, Fear, Laughter and Tears

"We learn, grow and become compassionate and generous as much through exile as homecoming, as much through loss as gain, as much through giving things away as in receiving what we believe to be our due."

– David Whyte

A Journey of Hope in Bad Times and Good

Journal - End of March through December 2020

Dear reader and friend, I don't know when you first discovered this book of hope. If COVID-19 is still around, please keep faith that it will be over soon. Try to be patient a little while longer. Everyone needs a megadose of patience, kindness, empathy and compassion right now. Please spread it around. If you lost loved ones during the pandemic, my heart goes out to you. Stay *in* life, remember the best of who they were, and know that their spirit is *always* with you. If the pandemic is finally over, I hope that you and your family are feeling well physically, emotionally and mentally. If not, please reach out to others for support, emotional sustenance and love. Above all, keep faith, stay strong, and believe in miracles and the healing power of love.

Even though this journal shares my good, bad, and funny experiences, thoughts and feelings during COVID-19, its purpose is much deeper. Metaphorically, COVID-19 symbolizes any crisis that unexpectedly changes our lives. How can we find our way towards hope amid all the darkness? How can we keep our lives together when everything feels like it's falling apart? During the long months, not only did we experience the coronavirus, but we were also shocked by a video that captured a white police officer callously murdering yet another black human being. In fact, he was one of 164 other black people who had met the same fate in the first eight months of 2020. The rage I felt in seeing this video forced me to ask introspective questions about myself and introspective questions about systemic racism and what can be done about it. As if that wasn't enough to handle emotionally, the political and social polarization in our country created an undercurrent of anxiety in my body, mind and spirit every day and all day. I'm sure I wasn't alone in feeling it. I kept asking myself, "Despite all our differences, why can't we be respectful to each other? Why is it so difficult for people to realize that we are more alike than different? Why is there so much animosity and violence? There must be a way to find common ground, unify our country, and see all our brothers and sisters through the eyes of love."

Sprinkled in-between the serious topics are funny COVID-19 stories, jokes, reflections, insights and personal situations. I also share my delight at all the small things that suddenly gave me joy and profound gratefulness. Thank you for taking the time to read my thoughts while reflecting on the ups and downs in your own life, too.

Love, Fears, Laughter and Tears

Humor and the pandemic. Love and fear. Peace and chaos. Strength and grief. Hope and trauma. Empathy and apathy. Laughter and tears. Compassion and indifference. Isn't it amazing how many contradictory feelings exist at the same moment or in the same day?

Journal Entry - March. At first, the stay-at-home order seemed like the promise of a fun staycation, but as time went by, harsh reality set in. Still, I think our personal situation was easy. Our children were grown, we're retired, and it's just the two of us at home. Because of our ages and Barry's history of heart disease, we had one goal. *Don't catch COVID-19.* Our motto? "Stay Safe." That's it.

Journal Entry - April: I wanted to take a walk as a form of aerobic exercise, but something made me stop short today. It was a simple bud on a tree. It called my name and asked me to take a closer look at its beauty. I had a mask on my face, but it seemed as if the mask allowed me to see the buds on the trees even more clearly than before. How is this possible? I am not sure if I have ever noticed the gradual unfolding of Spring before this moment. I must have been too busy multi-tasking. I guess it took a pandemic to wake me up. I feel as if I am one heartbeat with Spring and can notice every sight, sound and smell with new awareness. Each bud dances toward my eyes in full dimension, inviting me to breathe in its beauty and say to the universe, "thank you." I feel like a newborn baby who observes color, sound, shape and dimension with wonder, and for dessert, when I look up at the sky, I am delighted more than usual by its unlimited expanse and beauty.

As bad as life is right now, it feels surprisingly good.

Another gift. Unexpected laughter. People are generously posting COVID-19 videos and jokes online and they are all genuinely funny. I've had great big belly laughs. In fact, I've laughed so hard, tears rolled down my face. Despite a world on edge, the pandemic inspired an endless flow of creativity and humor, and even though I felt like crying, it felt good to laugh instead.

Here are some of my favorite jokes ...

- *Remember when we were little and had underwear with the names of the days of the week on them?*
  I need them now.
- *I need to get out of this bed! I'm late for the couch.*
- (During the toilet paper shortage) *Ran out of toilet paper and now using lettuce leaves. Today was just the tip of the iceberg. Tomorrow romaines to be seen.*
- *I used to spin that toilet paper like I was on "Wheel of Fortune." Now, I turn it like I'm cracking a safe.*
- *I need to practice social distancing from the refrigerator.*
- *Public Service Announcement - Every few days, try your jeans on just to make sure they fit. Pajamas will have you believe all is well in the kingdom.*
- *This morning I saw a neighbor talking to her cat. It was obvious she thought her cat understood her. I came into my house and told my dog. We laughed a lot.*

Journal Entry - May: I'm writing in my "Grateful Journal" much more these days, and as a result, I'm feeling more centered, at peace, less anxious, and deeply grateful for all the small and big miracles of life. What am I grateful for? Love. My husband. Our children. Our grandchildren. My sister. My extended family. Old friends. New friends. Good health. My home. Food. Nature. Music. The dedication and deep caring that all our healthcare professionals, first responders and essential frontline workers offer us every day. The kindness and heroism of strangers. Despite all the COVID-19 challenges in Italy, a video on television showed heart-centered people singing to each other on their balconies. It was an act of love, connection and caring that made humanity shine and gave me faith in the goodness of people. My *Shift of Heart* Facebook community. The peace podcast I was featured on with Barbara Gaughen-Muller. The Visioneers International Network. It is all food for my soul. Ah, yes. That beautiful flower over there. The birds at my feeder and their sweet songs. And that sunset last night! Wow! Did you see it, too?

> *Gratefulness feeds our spirit and reminds us that the greatest joys in life are often found in the simple things.*

To my reader: The next date in my journal, May 25, 2020, focuses on the murder of a black man. My anger is palpable. You may remember the day, too. His name was and is George Perry Floyd, Jr.

Journal Entry - May 25: I feel sick to my stomach. Just when I thought life couldn't get any worse, it did. It is a murder that has been committed many times, but because of all the recorded footage and the far-reaching power of social media, this murder seems to be shaking the nation more than usual. I watched the news in absolute horror as a white police officer forcefully pushed one of his knees into the neck of an unarmed black man. The black man's name is George Perry Floyd, Jr.

His family lovingly called Floyd their "gentle giant." In the video, I could hear him cry, "Officer, I can't breathe. I can't breathe." The officer, along with three assisting officers, completely ignored all his cries for help, and seven minutes and forty-six seconds later, the "gentle giant" died on a street in Minneapolis, Minnesota.

Why are these crimes still taking place in the *United* States of America, our land of liberty and *one* nation for *all*? People of every color are protesting in the streets day after day and night after night. Despite COVID-19 and the use of tear gas, rubber bullets, pepper spray, stingball grenades, horses, shields and batons, nothing stopped all the heartfelt pleas for racial justice. After four hundred years of racial discrimination, the Black Lives Matter movement inspired the world to awaken to a new consciousness. I hope it will last.

Recently, I heard Liseli A. Fitzpatrick, a Wellesley College professor and a powerful poet, read her heart-wrenching poem about racial injustice. I felt pain in my soul when I heard her words ...

we've been here before
(The 1619 Project)

we've been here
before bound
face to face
with the unknown
> shoved into tight
> spaces, shackled,
> strangled by the
> suffocating,
> un-sanitized
> stench of capitalism and
> communicable diseases
> unable to breathe
> muzzled behind iron-masks
> savagely uprooted and s c a t t e r e d
> across   sugar plantations   and   white   cotton fields
> forced to reimagine home
> in slums and shanties
> with no running water or
> happy birthday songs
> to wash our hands
> or toilet paper
> or food
> because
> we could not
> eat what we
> reaped
> gathered bones
> black and brown
> bodies thrown into

unmarked graves
    we were here before
    carried in the resilient
    blood of our ancestors
    who with girded loins
    transported us across
    their backs dismantling
    systems with their own tools
    quilting fabrics from scraps
    Soul-stirring delicacies like songs
divining
altars and organs
in their lungs
    because,
    the *earth is a tabernacle*
    and the body   an instrument
    and the heart   a beat
    and God only comes alive
when we dance
we've been here
before
standing on
the shoulders
of the ancestors
who taught us
    how to make
something
out of nothing
and summon
light out of darkness
fear not, we've been here before

            – by Liseli A. Fitzpatrick

Police officers aren't the only ones who stereotype, profile and discriminate. Prejudice is everywhere. We are all accountable for each word, action, reaction, thought and feeling rooted in any kind of prejudice. Anyone who is courageous enough to take a hard and honest look at themselves can make a conscious and life-changing decision to shift their mindset to one of inclusion, respect and empathy. It is never too late. We have the power to change the way we react to each other. We have the power to shift our hearts to love.

Journal Entry - Beginning of June: I keep finding small rocks on the ground with power words painted on them. *Love. Hope. Faith. Trust. Believe.* Yesterday, I saw rocks with painted butterflies, peace signs and rainbows. I wonder who implemented this sweet act of kindness? Whoever you are, thank you. I love rocks. Any size. Any shape. I love holding a rock in the palm of my hand when I speak with someone or think about something. A rock is soothing, steady, present, solid, and gives me comfort at a time of little control and constant change. I have always collected rocks and own big jars of them in my home. Each rock reminds me of a trip I experienced somewhere on this beautiful earth. I know I can't travel right now, but each rock reminds me of the places I've been lucky enough to visit.

Journal Entry - End of June: Our little Saturday night "adventure" took place after all the retail stores were closed for the day. In a desperate need for random entertainment, we drove to a neighboring town. When we arrived in front of my two favorite stores, I ran out of the car to look in the windows. My jaw dropped when I saw the aisles and aisles of clothes, pocketbooks and home decorations, and lo and behold, I had an unexpected meltdown. Not just any meltdown. An "ugly tears" kind of meltdown. Seeing my old life in front of me hurt. I miss the freedom to casually browse in stores, eat in restaurants, give family and friends hugs, go to my local library, see a live concert or play, travel, enjoy the beach, get my hair done. The list is endless. I miss it all.

> *Okay, stop. COVID-19 won't last forever. We made a conscious decision to keep our risk level to an absolute minimum and that's what we are doing. Above all else, we do not want to be another COVID-19 statistic. It's worth the small sacrifices we are making to stick with our plan. I am determined to be positive and grateful, no matter what. I have it all.*

Journal Entry - July: I am probably one of the few people who feels that it's not safe to go into a grocery store. I order all my groceries online and rely on my hardworking Instacart shopper to find all my groceries and bring them to my home. We text each other to make sure that all my preferences are clear. In reviewing one of my texts, it appears to have an air of bossiness, but in my defense, grocery shopping has always been one of my favorite chores. I miss choosing my groceries in person. The text was my feeble attempt to gain a semblance of control in a situation in which there is little control.

Thank you for doing the grocery shopping for me. I really appreciate it. Please make sure that the bananas aren't too soft, brown, or overly green - just a little green; make sure my items have long expiration dates; make sure that you choose fruits with no bruises; most of all, please make sure my ice cream doesn't melt. In fact, could you purchase my ice cream just before you check out and place it in my cart last?

Journal Entry - July 29: It wasn't my idea of fun to have my birthday during a pandemic. I miss traveling to Ogunquit and walking on the beach at low tide. I love sleeping overnight at a motel, chatting with Barry as we walk hand-in-hand on Marginal Way, slurping ice cream together, browsing in stores, and exploring all the different restaurants.

I took so many things for granted.

Journal Entry - July 29 (evening): I've had wonderful birthdays in my life, but for some reason, this birthday was one of the best. It began with breakfast in bed, then heartwarming FaceTime chats with family and friends, and ended with a picnic at a secluded lake just as the sun was setting. We even stayed for the afterglow.

It was a day full of simple delights and the healing power of love.

Journal Entry - August: Because my car has been sitting in the garage for weeks, I decided that today was the day to start up the engine and spruce up on my driving skills. As I was drove down Route 9, I noticed a large sign in front of one of my favorite stores that said, "Aisle. One Way."

Hmm. What's an aisle? I don't remember any more. I haven't been part of an aisle since March. As strange as it feels to say this, I crave being part of an aisle. In fact, I would be ecstatic to be part of a group of people who are standing in line for a common purpose. It's funny how I used to take a simple thing like "aisles" for granted. Now, my life is an aisle of two - my husband and me. I wonder if I can call all the people that I see in the Zoom windows a certain type of "aisle." In a strange way, it might make me feel better. More "normally abnormal." Oh, for an aisle!

Journal Entry - August 6: It's our anniversary. In the "good old days," we would have dressed up and made reservations to eat at our favorite restaurant. I wish we were brave enough to eat on their patio today, but we aren't. It's not worth the stress to think that we might catch COVID-19.

Journal Entry - August 6 (later that evening): Another special day. The morning began with a gift of gorgeous roses from my honey, a long relaxing walk at a beautiful state park, and then when we returned home, we had warm talks on FaceTime with family and friends. For dinner, we picked up Italian food from a local restaurant. I set a fancy table, put the food in the microwave to destroy any chance of breathing in COVID-19 germs, lit the candles and the butterfly lamp, put on relaxing Hawaiian music, and had the best time in the world.

Just like my birthday, it was a day full of simple delights and the healing power of love.

Journal Entry – Beginning of September: During COVID-19, people made questionable choices that triggered my inner judge.

How can people think and act this way? Why don't they wear a face mask and physically distance? Why are they still gathering in large groups? Why don't they care about the collective whole? Why can't we be on the same page? What about social responsibility? Why can't we find it in our hearts to support, care and love all our brothers and sisters? Why is it so difficult to live the wisdom of "love thy neighbor as thyself?"

- **Question to self.** How can I let go of my inner judge and shift my heart from fear and judgment to compassion, empathy and love?

What I am about to write is an emotional stretch and perhaps my biggest spiritual challenge. I do not support violence, hatred, bigotry, discrimination, bias and injustice of any kind. Still, I believe that I need to find a way to embody the spirit of an inclusive love towards all human beings, no matter what someone has done or said. That doesn't mean that I approve of their life choices in any way. It just means that I can separate their actions from my desire to see all human beings with love.

Everyone has a life story that helped shape their thoughts, words, actions and reactions. Many behaviors have been passed down from generation to generation. Do I have it in me to send them thoughts of healing, transformation, love and light, no matter what they did? Do I have it in me to remember their pure child-heart that lives underneath all the chaos? After all, we are born open-minded, loving and innocent. No one is born violent and bigoted. Bigotry is passed down and there are deep-seated reasons why violence, discrimination and hatred are part of someone's life. The choices we find ourselves making in our lives are often based on fear or based on love. If I can remember that most choices and behaviors are based around these two emotional reactions, it might help to shift my own thoughts, feelings and behaviors from the energy of fear to the energy of unconditional love.

I had a heart-to-heart with my inner judge and created a new intention. I will do my best to surround each person on this earth with light. I don't need to agree with them, and they don't need to agree with me. Everyone has a basic need for empathy, healing and love. I will continue to work hard to release my inner judge, open to the softness of unconditional love, and make a conscious choice to "love my neighbor as myself." No college degree required.

Journal Entry – End of September: I've been thinking about the last six months. Different people. Different reactions. Once the stay-at-home advisory ended, there were still people who chose to stay close to home. Like me, for example. It's been six months since I've been to a hairdresser, eaten in restaurants, seen my grandchildren in person, shopped or traveled. I think I deserve a gold sticker and a large trophy that says, "Most Stoic, Most Scared and Most Cautious." Other people decided to be less cautious. They made conscious choices to take measured risks. They wore face masks, shopped for groceries, got their hair cut, enjoyed manicures, ate in restaurants, met with friends, took short trips, and browsed in stores. Still others didn't seem to care about the concept of "risk versus benefit." They couldn't handle staying home for one more second, and when the stay-at-home order ended, they flew out the door and never looked back. I wish they had weighed the cause and effect of some of their choices more carefully, but their reactions are understandable. We are all tired of being cooped up. Psychologists call it "COVID-19 fatigue."

Adapting to the abnormal as normal is never easy.

Journal Entry - October: It's the second wave of the COVID-19 and there is an uptick in cases and deaths every day. Some people wear face masks, and others don't. Businesses are closing, and hardworking people are losing their jobs and waiting in food lines with thousands of others. Some people question the value of science, health experts, governors and mayors are being threatened by those who don't agree with their decisions, some political rallies require physical distancing and mask wearing, other political rallies do not, and there is a heated presidential election just around the corner.

The last seven months have been incredibly stressful. In fact, it has been stressful longer than that. Everyone seems to have a different opinion about the importance of wearing a face mask, physical distancing, hybrid versus remote learning, opening schools, bars and restaurants, COVID-19 testing and tracing, coronavirus vaccinations, the Black Lives Matter movement, racial profiling, police brutality, defunding the police, the value of science, the definition of fake news, the validity of religious discrimination, gender bias, the Deferred Action for Childhood Arrivals movement (DACA), Pro-Life versus Pro-Choice, the Affordable Care Act, and the fate of all the children of immigrants who have been mercilessly forced to separate from their families.

There are also different opinions and biases about unemployment, poverty, homelessness, food shortages, Russian interference, the sanctity of our democracy, social media, frequent fires on the

West Coast, truth and muzzling the truth, political pressure that may be influencing the accuracy of information provided by the Centers for Disease Control and Prevention, the United States Food and Drug Administration, and the National Institutes of Health, the importance of the World Health Organization, the use of military force to stop peaceful protests, the removal of Confederate flags and monuments, the protection of our environment, the removal of mailboxes and sorting machines to impede voting, the validity of global warming, the Second Amendment, and controversial discussions on the definition of free speech.

> *Every issue is important to me and every injustice is unacceptable. I need to do my part to help make this world a more loving and compassionate place. There is no time to lose.*

Journal Entry - November: The months have flown by and the months have dragged on. It seems impossible that both time warps exist simultaneously, but they do, and unless I glance at my iPhone, I have no idea what day it is. I think I'm numb, tired, traumatized and scared, and I know I'm not the only one who feels this way. As an empath, I can sense all the stress, anxiety, depression, loneliness, fear, egocentricity, altruism, frustration, confusion, caring, pain, suffering, anger, grief, determination, kindness, strength, faith, love, optimism, heartbreak and hope in the air.

Despite everything, I am feeling profoundly grateful. Grateful that my family is still safe; grateful to all our first responders and healthcare workers for their incredible dedication, determination, resilience, courage and sacrifice; grateful to all the essential frontline workers who work hard to keep our lives running as smoothly as possible; grateful to every parent who valiantly tries to keep everyone in their "bubble" safe and secure; grateful to every dedicated, flexible, hardworking and caring teacher; grateful to every generous person and organization who offered online concerts, stimulating classes, peace and justice gatherings, quality workshops, calming meditations, yoga classes, sound healing experiences, life coaching, aerobic classes, art, music, plays, virtual Broadway shows, lessons, lectures, museum tours, virtual travel experiences, spiritual services, special gatherings, seminars and conferences.

Most of all, I am grateful to Dr. Anthony S. Fauci, the Director of The National Institute of Allergy and Infectious Diseases for his scientific expertise, calm presence amid all the chaos, anger and confusion, and for taking the high road by showing impeccable dignity, integrity and grace in the face of adversity.

Journal Entry - December 11: **Hope.** The Federal Food and Drug Administration took action in the fight against the novel coronavirus by granting emergency use authorization for Pfizer's COVID-19 Vaccine. Healthcare workers will be inoculated first and those in long-term care facilities will be inoculated next. I know it will take months to vaccinate the rest of the population, but we are finally on our way out of this nightmare.

Journal Entry - December 17: **Hope.** The Federal Food and Drug Administration granted emergency use authorization for Moderna's COVID-19 Vaccine.

There are no adequate words to express my deepest gratitude to all the scientists who worked with such passion and focus to make this happen. When the pandemic is finally over, what do I want to remember? What do you want to remember? What did we learn? What do we appreciate now that we didn't appreciate before? How have we changed?

CHAPTER SIX

Inner Peace, Healing, Loving and Living - Part II

"Decide to be happy
Render others happy
Proclaim your joy
Love passionately your miraculous life
Do not listen to promises
Do not wait for a better world
Be grateful for every moment of life."

– Dr. Robert Muller, former Assistant Secretary-General of the United Nations

Most of All They Taught Me Happiness

Transformational Tools in Bad Times and Good

"Let tenderness pour from your eyes, the way the sun gazes warmly on earth."

– Hafez

Whether I'm in the middle of a crisis or my life is smooth as butter, I reach for my smorgasbord of "peace begins with me" healing techniques. Every self-care strategy can be a remedy for turning self-made chaos into the calm of inner peace.

After all, if I'm a chaotic mess, how will I be able to offer peace and love to others? How will you?

Transformational Tools for Inner Peace, Healing, Loving and Living

Close your eyes, stop the world, put your hand on your heart, and simply breathe. When I am stressed, I return to my favorite transformational tool. I close my eyes, turn off the noise, put my hand on my heart, and simply breathe. That's it. It's a self-care strategy that seems like a no-brainer, but many of us dismiss its importance. Luckily, I now realize the wondrous power of this tool. This one simple approach connects us to our body, our heart, and the breath of the universe. The most effective ideas are usually the purest ones. Return to this technique many times a day.

The quality of each breath. Be mindful of the quality of every breath. Is your breathing shallow and fast? Deep and slow? If your breathing is shallow, take breaths that are longer, slower and deeper. Before long, you will be able to feel your entire body shift into a relaxing inner sigh. *"Ahh. Peace at last."*

The healing power of words. For dessert, I add the healing power of words to my "close your eyes, stop the world, place your hand on your heart, and simply breathe" meditation. With every inhale, I think the words, *deep peace, let go and trust.* With every exhale, I think the words, *deep peace, let go and trust.*

Keep your body moving. Even if you aren't into exercise, add the joy of "freedom dancing" to your day. Put on relaxing music, close your eyes, and let the music move your body. Next, put on music that energizes you. If you are a person with a physical disability, use the power of your mind to imagine dancing to your heart's delight. I was once told by a professor of music and dance that our subconscious mind can't discern whether we are truly dancing or imagining it. See yourself dancing on the ocean shore or on top of a mountain. As you see yourself in your mind's eye, freedom, healing and relaxation will fill your entire being. In bad times and good, move. End your freedom dance with relaxation music and add meditative gratefulness, stillness, breath and quiet to your free movement finale.

Positive Self-talk. There are times when I say good things to myself, and there are times when I don't. There are moments when I know my value, the qualities I am inspired to offer the world, am confident, secure, determined, courageous, strong, and my heart overflows with peace and love. There are other moments when I am my own worst critic, berate myself, am fearful, insecure, anxious, and wonder if there will ever be a world of peace, unity and love.

There are also days when I am a combination of both positive and negative thinking. I am a smattering of pessimistic Eeyore from the book, *Winnie-the-Pooh*, and a smattering of the more optimistic Tigger, Winnie-the-Pooh, Owl, Christopher Robin, Rabbit, Kanga, Roo, and Piglet. Because personality traits, noisy inner voices and varied feelings often collide with each other, it is normal to vacillate between both optimism and pessimism. That said, it is still important to be mindful of the quality of every thought ...

> *Is this thought a weed that needs to be discarded, released and pulled out from its root, or is it a sunflower gradually unfolding into its full potential? If we are mostly critical, snarly, and "glass half empty" thinkers, it would be beneficial to shift our disgruntled attitude as quickly as possible. After all, too many weeds in our garden of life will keep the sunlight from shining and our life from blossoming to its full potential.*

Positive self-talk transcends insecurities and fears and encourages us to acknowledge the best of who we are. Now and then, look at yourself in the mirror with warm and loving eyes. Acknowledge your strength and beauty. It isn't boastful. It isn't narcissistic. It is loving, compassionate, caring, supportive, forgiving and healing.

"You know what? I love you, flaws and all. I know you try your best, and as Maya Angelou said, "when you know better, you do better." What strength! What courage! What resilience! Look at all the tremendous challenges you experienced in your life. You never gave up. You never give up. I'm so proud of you. Hi, my friend. My best friend. Let's do something positive together. Let's see. What gives you joy? Laughter? Relaxation? Peace? Whatever you need to heal your spirit, let's do it. Above all, keep moving forward with love in your heart and peace in your soul. Don't allow the naysayers and pessimists of the world sway you from your path of love. Give yourself permission to enjoy more of your time on earth. Follow your dreams every step of the way and invite your highest intuition to guide all your choices. Make it your intention to find a way to uplift your spirit, and while you're at it, make it your intention to uplift someone else's spirit, too.

Best friends forever. When my inner critic is the only voice I hear, I know it's time to return to my positive self-talk technique again. Instead of being my own worst enemy, I shift to being my own best friend. While addressing my alter ego, I assume two roles. I am the person who has a problem, and I am also the person who has the power to be her own inner guru, life coach and best friend.

Melody, I know you're going through a difficult challenge and you're not sure how to handle it. Let me ask you a question. If a friend had to face a challenge like yours, what would you say or do to help? I don't know why, but it's always so much easier to suggest just the right remedy to a friend. After you hear the wisdom you gave "your best friend," offer yourself the same advice. One of the pearls of wisdom I told "my best friend" focused on the healing power of words. I inspired her to say ...

"I can handle this situation. Step by step and breath by breath, I have the strength to deal with anything that comes my way. I've proven my inner strength before and I will prove it again. I can do this!"

So, dear reader. Are you ready? Say hello to your beautiful essence. Your best friend. Cherish, respect and honor yourself. Offer yourself the same wisdom, guidance, compassion, forgiveness, kindness and love you offer others. What would you say to your friend? Give yourself the same pep talk.

The healing energy in one special rock. Babies love holding an object that makes them feel secure and calm. Adults often need a strategy like this, too. Take a rock, for example. My rock isn't just any rock. It's a special rock. As I go through my day, you might notice me holding an oval-shaped rock in the palm of one of my hands. I feel its weight and notice a strong vibration that resonates through the rock and into my body. Just like a baby who holds a lovey for comfort, the vibration of this rock comforts and grounds me, too. I feel more relaxed, my words flow more easily, I can listen to a friend's heart with focused attention, I am more connected to the earth, my thoughts are clear, and it is a great addition to the "close your eyes, stop the world, put your hand on your heart, and simply breathe" approach. I hold other objects, too. A healing crystal, a heart-opening amethyst, a beautiful shell, a delicate flower.

Look around. What do you see? Are you drawn towards a certain object? Which one seems to vibrate comfort, positive energy, confidence and strength? Look at everything in your home and look outside, too. Is there a sacred object you can hold in the palm of your hand that might help you feel more connected with yourself and the universe?

Love is a decision. When my husband and I were first married, we wanted to get off to a good start by registering for a workshop on the art of giving and receiving love. As I looked at the hand-out, I read an affirmation that confused me. It said, "love is a decision." As I listened to the facilitators talk about love, I couldn't stop my inner judge from rattling away. "What? Isn't love about the heart? What are they talking about?" Years later, I understood. Love can dissipate, feel shaky and unsure.

When you don't feel the kind of love you usually feel, it can be scary. If your relationship is generally healthy and you have the potential to grow and learn together, this is the moment when you need to make a conscious decision with your mind to trust in the ebb and flow of love. When the timing is right, you will feel it again. Meanwhile, *decide* to trust in the power of love. When you least expect it, love will resonate in your heart once again.

Peace is a decision. As much as we believe in peace, unpeaceful people and their actions often take center stage. When hope for a world of peace becomes challenging to your soul, walk the path of peace anyway. Make a conscious decision to be a peacebuilder. No matter what!

Look within. As you know, inner inquiry is one of my favorite techniques. When I ask soul-searching questions, it stimulates my curiosity about the unknown parts of myself, and after I ask the universe my questions, I listen. When I hear the wisdom whispers, I turn to my journal and document what I just heard and felt.

What questions would you like to ask your heart, inner voice, highest wisdom and intuition? Trust. The answers will come. Let's invite the process of inner inquiry into your life ...

- *How can I respond to difficult challenges with more patience, strength, courage and grace?*

  _____

  _____

  _____

- *How can I learn to live with chaos and calm in parallel with each other?*

  _____

  _____

  _____

- *Which self-care healing strategies are helping me the most?*

_____

_____

_____

- *How can I walk the path of peace and love amid the chaos of adversity?*

_____

_____

_____

- *How can I BE the peace I want in the world?*

_____

_____

_____

Embody the spirit of hope. Be patient. Inner growth and positive transformation take a lifetime. Do the inner work required to take care of yourself, and if you need extra support, please don't hesitate to reach out to a good therapist. As the saying goes, "secure your own oxygen mask first before assisting others." Above all, never give up. You have the power to make it through anything and everything, and when you least expect it, hope will dance in your heart once again.

Good-for-your-soul lyrics. In *Peace Dreamer*, it is my delight to share some of my original song lyrics with you. Do you enjoy music, too? Have you found meaningful songs that contain lyrics that inspire you to live your life with inner peace, love, strength and hope? Make a list of all the songs that inspire you, and when you're feeling blue, you'll know exactly what to do.

Self-Care Reminders: A Summary

"The art of being happy lies in the power of
extracting happiness from common things."

– Henry Ward Beecher

*Which tools for self-care and
healing will you choose today?*

- Stop the world.

- Close your eyes.

- Put your hand on your heart, stay in the present, and
  breathe.

- Inhale and exhale deeply.

- Inhale and exhale slowly.

- Be fully present. Here. Now. This moment.

- When you listen to someone's heart, offer them your
  complete undivided presence. No cell phones. No other
  distractions. Just the beauty and vulnerability of that
  person and you. It is a magnificent gift of the heart and
  to the heart.

- Add freedom dancing to your life.

- Invent power words, mantras and positive affirmations.

- Write your power words down. Think them. Sing them. Say them out loud.

- Use the creative arts as a form of self-expression and healing.

- Give without expecting anything in return.

- Open your heart towards receiving all the good that life has to offer.

- Visualize a greater feeling of peace and healing inside yourself.

- Visualize the possibility of peace in the world.

- Send the power of love, healing, kindness and light to others.

- Inspire.

- Trust.

- Keep Faith.

- Hold a sacred object in the palm of your hand and allow its vibrations to ground you.

- Look within.

- Ask the universe soul-searching questions.

- Keep your mind open.

- Keep your heart open.

- Meditate.

- Pray in your own way.

- Listen to life's wisdom whispers.

- Write all your feelings and thoughts down in a journal.

- Shift to positive self-talk.

- Ask the highest part within yourself, "What wisdom would I give to a good friend?" Give yourself the same suggestion.

- Fight for yourself.

- Never give up.

- Stay strong, determined and persistent.

- Become your own best friend.

- Reach out to a therapist for extra support.

- Integrate at least one "peace begins with me" self-care strategy every day.

- Listen to songs that empower your life.

- Remember that there is always hope in bad times and good.

In moments when I quietly wonder if peace will happen in my lifetime, I turn to this song. Every word is purposefully designed to rekindle the promise and commitment of hope, love and peace.

Three Words

From the album, *Listen to the Whispers*

Hope is the feeling to keep inside of you
Love is the answer with our words and with what we do
Peace is the vision we must imagine near
Keep these three words in your heart clear.

Hope, love, peace is the way
Hope, love, peace is the way.

When the world feels too heavy to bear in your soul
And your heart is on empty and you feel far from whole
When you're feeling angry, confused or alone ...

Just remember these three words to come home to yourself
Remember these three words to come home.

Hope, love, peace is the way
Hope, love, peace is the way.

CHAPTER SEVEN

Ancient Healing Techniques for Modern Times

A "Peace Begins with Me" Toolkit

"Fear is the cheapest room in the house. I would like to see you living in better conditions."

– Hafez

Chakras Made Easy

"Revving up your chakras will help you live your
time on earth with inner peace, sunshine, happiness,
confidence, strength, courage, healing, hope, light
and love."

– Cheryl Melody Baskin

I am a cheerleader for self-care, healing, personal growth and transformation. Why? As changemakers, we need to create a continuous flow of positive energy. We don't want to burn out. The world needs us.

When I first heard about the mysterious world of chakras, I was awed by its ancient history. Although the concept was initially out of comfort zone, when I learned that the chakra system originated in India between 1500 and 500 BC, this fact alone inspired me to give it further attention, curiosity and respect. Along with mindfulness meditation and yoga, chakra balancing is considered one of the most effective tools for transformational healing. Curiosity and respect propelled me to personally experience its benefits, and after using the chakra energy balancing technique for over thirty years, I am a passionate advocate.

How does the chakra energy balancing technique relate to a book on peace, love, healing and hope? Buried deep within each of the seven chakras, there are inner child wounds, everyday emotions, physical pain and negative core beliefs. When I sense a need for added healing, confidence, strength, energy, grounding, trust and an overall tune-up, I turn to the chakra energy balancing technique for support, a renewed feeling of well-being and deep personal insight. It is one of the best tools I know for honoring the phrase, "peace begins with me."

What is a chakra? "Chakra" is a Sanskrit word that means "wheel of spinning energy." A chakra is a whirling power of vibration located in an area of the body that connects to the flow of life. It is often referred to as a wheel, circle, disk, vortex or energy center. By revving up the energy field in each of your seven chakras, many of the wounds we carry around with us every day soften. Because most of us live with inner issues that remain unhealed, some chakras spin more vibrantly than others. When your chakras spin fully, they ground your body, lighten your energy, open your heart, increase stamina, reinforce strength and courage, create positive core beliefs, heal inner wounds, support you in actualizing your dreams, free your voice, help gain clarity, access your highest intuition, and most of all, shift fear into the energy of love.

What do you need for your chakra journey? Imagination, intuition and trust. Just like other spiritual concepts that can't be seen by the naked eye and can only be sensed, it is our intuition, not the human eye, that can see, sense and feel chakras.

Once I learned where the seven chakras were located, their individual colors and each chakra's metaphorical meaning, I found that the chakra energy balancing technique was almost better than a cup of coffee. I use my intuition to assess the health of each chakra, and then after my assessment, I focus on one or more of my chakras before getting out of bed in the morning, in the shower, and throughout my day. It may take as little as five minutes to feel a renewed sense of healing and balance, or if I need more time, I will create a space in my life to use the chakra energy balancing approach for thirty minutes or more.

My teaching philosophy. When I teach, I enjoy incorporating a variety of healing tools. I know that everyone has a different learning style. Some of us learn better through visual or auditory methods, while others learn best through touch (hands-on), or by using bodily-kinesthetic movement. If one method doesn't work, something else will. In this case, "less isn't more." More is more.

For example, throughout your experiential process, I will ask you to move your hand counterclockwise above one of your chakras for a few minutes, and then change directions and move your hand clockwise for a few minutes. When your hand is moving counterclockwise, you are drawing negative energy out and away from your chakra, and when your hand is moving clockwise, you are rebalancing, healing and smoothing your chakra. I will also ask you to multi-task. Each chakra contains a metaphorical meaning. When you are rebalancing your first chakra with good energy, for example, I will ask you to visualize the qualities of courage and confidence. I will also add positive affirmations, sound healing, heart-dreaming, bodily-kinesthetic movement, meditations and guided visualizations to our chakra journey.

First things, first. Let's begin our "peace begins with me" chakra journey with a basic introduction.

Our Seven Chakras

"Every artist dips his brush into his own soul and
paints his own nature into his pictures."

– Henry Ward Beecher

Believe it or not, your body contains 114 chakras. To make your
chakra energy balancing experience relaxing, joyful, effective
and user-friendly, we will only focus on seven ...

Your first chakra is also called the root chakra. It spins at
the base of your spine, the pelvic floor, the first three vertebrae,
the bladder, and the soles of your feet. The color associated with
the first chakra is **red.**

Your second chakra is also called the sacral chakra.
It spins above the pubic bone and below the navel. The color
associated with the second chakra is **orange.**

Your third chakra is also called the solar plexus. It spins
from your navel to your ribcage. The color associated with the
third chakra is **yellow.**

Your fourth chakra is also called the heart center. It is
the bridge between the first three lower chakras and the upper
chakras. It lies in the center of your chest and involves the
thymus gland, lungs and breasts. The color associated with the
fourth chakra is **emerald green.**

Your fifth chakra is also called the throat chakra. It spins around the throat area, thyroid, parathyroid, jaw, neck, mouth, tongue and larynx. The color associated with the fifth chakra is **sky blue.**

Your sixth chakra is also called the third eye energy center. It is located between your two eyebrows, and it is also associated with your pituitary gland, eyes, head and the lower part of your brain. The color associated with the sixth chakra is **indigo.**

Your seventh chakra is also called the crown chakra. It spins at the top of your head. The colors associated with the seventh chakra are **violet** and **white.**

Creative Visualization and Chakra Balancing

"There are painters who transform the sun to a yellow spot, but there are others who, with the help of their art and their intelligence, transfer a yellow spot into the sun."

— Pablo Picasso

Let's go on a vacation together. To get ready to experience the full impact of the chakra energy balancing technique, let's activate our ability to imagine, create, sense, intuit and visualize. I have a feeling that creative visualization is part of what you already do to honor your dreams. Whether my hunch is accurate or not, taking a little time out to visualize various scenes in our mind's eye is like going on a free vacation without lugging heavy suitcases, running to your next flight or finding comfortable lodging.

Experiential Activities

Visualization is an inner muscle that needs constant exercise. In the following visualization exercises, read one of the sentences, close your eyes, imagine the scene, linger there for awhile, and then, when you feel ready, move onto the next sentence.

- Imagine walking barefoot on the beach at low tide. After you imagine this scene for awhile, "try" to let it go.

When you can pull yourself away, get ready to picture a new scene.

- Breathe in the smell of freshly baked bread.

- Touch the bark of a redwood tree.

- Watch a colorful butterfly flutter around the purple and yellow flowers.

- See yourself standing on a mountaintop.

- See yourself paddling a yellow and orange kayak on a smooth and glistening lake.

- Eat a mouthwatering dessert.

- Write your name on the sidewalk using three different colors of chalk.

- Watch the rising sun.

- Follow a rainbow.

- The day has finally come. A world of peace, unity, compassion, justice and love are part of every person on this earth. What does it look like? How are people celebrating? You worked hard for this day to come. Here it is. Only peace. Only love. Only unity. Only kindness. Only compassion. See it. Feel it. Breathe it into your soul. *Ahh.*

Let's Get Your Chakras Healing and Spinning!

"Passion and heart are not enough to accomplish all
the good things we want to do in life. We need it all!
We need strength, confidence, courage, stamina, big
dreams, fire, light, hope, clarity, power words, self-care,
love, compassion, intuition, wisdom and trust."

– Cheryl Melody Baskin

Now that your imagination is activated, it's time to take a deeper dive into the world of chakra balancing. If you would like to watch one of the many interpretations of this technique, please feel free to check out the "Chakras Made Easy" YouTube video: https://youtu.be/l9uPrRp4Z6E

Healing the First Chakra: This chakra is also called the root chakra. It spins at the base of your spine and the soles of your feet. Focus on expanding the energy of your first chakra and literally picture a "wheel of spinning energy." The first chakra is the home of stability, survival, rootedness, security, stamina, strength, grounding, letting go of fear, and feeling safe. Scan your first chakra and use your intuition to sense how it's doing. Is it vibrant, or does it need loving attention? Every dream you imagine for yourself and every dream you have for the world needs your first chakra to spin with strong and expansive vibrations. Place your hand slightly above this chakra and move it *counterclockwise* for a few minutes. Focus on clearing out anything that is blocking your growth. Stop, rub your hands together, shake out any negative energy, and breathe. Place your hand over your first chakra again, and this time move your hand *clockwise*. Focus on breathing in all the positive qualities that this chakra provides. Visualize walking in the world with more confidence, stamina and courage and feel the earth supporting you and giving you the gift of rooted strength.

Healing the Second Chakra: This chakra is also called the sacral chakra. It is located just below your navel. Focus on expanding the energy of your second chakra and literally picture a "wheel of spinning energy." The second chakra is the home of creative and sexual energy, and when this energy center is fully aligned and whirring, we are in the flow of life, passionate, confident, creative and spirited. We know our worth and our place in the world and we are excited to step into the life's unlimited potential. Scan your second chakra and use your highest intuition to sense how it's doing. Is it vibrant, or does it need more attention? Place your hand slightly above this chakra and move it *counterclockwise* for a few minutes. Focus on clearing out anything that is blocking your growth. Stop, rub your hands together, shake out any negative energy, and breathe. Place your hand over your second chakra again, and this time move your hand *clockwise*. Focus on breathing in all the positive qualities that this chakra provides. See yourself standing tall and taking your full space in the world. You are a child of the universe and have every right to be here. Every creative vision needs a healthy second chakra. Step fully into your dreams. No hiding. No making yourself small. Hold your head high. Honor your gifts and inspire others to reach for the stars, too.

Healing the Third Chakra: This chakra is also called the solar plexus. When the third chakra is aligned, we are full of zest, sparkle, sunshine, passion, light, and a commitment to living life to its fullest. Scan your third chakra and use your highest intuition to sense how it's doing. Is it vibrant, or does it need more attention? Place your hand slightly above this chakra and move it *counterclockwise* for a few minutes. Focus on clearing out anything that is blocking your growth. Stop, rub your hands together, shake out any negative energy, and breathe. Place your hand over your third chakra again, and this time move your hand *clockwise*. Focus on breathing in all the positive qualities that this chakra provides. Breathe in passion, a strong will to live, the glow of sunshine, the optimism of light, and your zest for celebrating every big and small joy in life. Call upon every inner growth tool available to ignite the flame of hope. Visualize, journal write, daydream, and keep putting one foot in front of the other as you actualize your biggest dreams.

Healing the Fourth Chakra: This chakra is in your heart space. The fourth chakra invites you to open your heart to love. Scan your heart chakra and use your highest intuition to sense how it's doing. Is it vibrant, or does it need more attention? Place your hand slightly above this chakra and move it *counterclockwise* for a few minutes. Focus on clearing out anything that is blocking your growth. Stop, rub your hands together, shake out any negative energy, and breathe. Place your hand over your fourth chakra again, and this time move your hand *clockwise*. Focus on breathing in all the positive qualities that this chakra provides. Your heart center focuses on the qualities of compassion, empathy, kindness and forgiveness. Even if you have been hurt in the past, try to open your heart just a little more towards love. Love is the path to healing and feeling alive. Love is the path to peace. Closing your heart will only shrink your capacity to feel joy. Return to the healing power of love.

Healing the Fifth Chakra: This chakra is also called the throat chakra. See yourself speaking up and sharing the heart of your truth. Scan your fifth chakra and use your highest intuition to sense how it's doing. Is it vibrant, or does it need more attention? Place your hand slightly above this chakra and move it *counterclockwise* for a few minutes. Focus on clearing out anything that is blocking your growth. Stop, rub your hands together, shake out any negative energy, and breathe. Place your hand over your fifth chakra again, and this time move your hand *clockwise*. Focus on breathing in all the positive qualities that this chakra provides. As you open the energy field of your fifth chakra, it is easier to share your truth with strength, clarity and love and to project the magnificence of who you are to the world. Even if there are naysayers in your life, release your voice. You have the power to inspire people and engage them in a new story of human consciousness. Give yourself a strong, confident, courageous, compassionate and wise voice in the world.

Healing the Sixth Chakra: This chakra is also called the third eye. It is located in the middle of your forehead and between both eyebrows. This is the sacred place of your highest intuition, wisdom and inner voice. Scan your sixth chakra and use your highest intuition to sense how it's doing. Is it vibrant, or does it need more attention? Place your hand slightly above this chakra and move it *counterclockwise* for a few minutes. Focus on clearing out anything that is blocking your growth. Stop, rub your hands together, shake out any negative energy, and breathe. Place your hand over your sixth chakra again, and this time move your hand *clockwise*. Focus on breathing in all the positive qualities that this chakra provides. If you would like to feel more in tune with the wisdom whispers of the universe, focus on expanding the energy field of the sixth chakra. Open this amazing energy center and imagine it spinning to its full capacity. The wisdom whispers echoed from your highest intuition will direct your life towards its greatest potential. Unknown coincidences, synchronicities and miracles will unfold when you least expect them.

Healing the Seventh Chakra: This chakra is also known as the crown or top of your head. This is the place where you feel loved and guided by an energy greater than yourself. Scan your seventh chakra and use your highest intuition to sense how it's doing. Is it vibrant, or does it need more attention? Place your hand slightly above this chakra and move it *counterclockwise* for a few minutes. Focus on clearing out anything that is blocking your growth. Stop, rub your hands together, shake out any negative energy, and breathe. Place your hand over your seventh chakra again, and this time move your hand *clockwise.* Focus on breathing in all the positive qualities that this chakra provides. The seventh chakra is the area of enlightenment, spiritual awakening and highest consciousness. As this chakra spins, you can feel a sense of oneness with the universe and are comforted by knowing that you are an integral part of the greater whole.

Once all seven chakras become your new best friends, it will only take a short time to rev them up. They have the power to shift your energy and attitude from fear to love, agitation to peace, weakness to strength, illness to wellness, timidity to courage. I like to think of our chakras as inner vortexes. If you have had the honor of visiting a vortex anywhere on this beautiful earth, you may remember its magnetic power. I still remember this power when I visited Bell Rock in Sedona, Arizona.

*Tuning up and healing each chakra
is like having Bell Rock inside us every day!
Let's do whatever we can to give ourselves
"Chakra Zing!"*

CHAPTER EIGHT

Calling All Dreamers

"Never give up on yourself and never give up on your dreams for a better world. When you least expect it, your life will shift. You will experience light on your face and hope in your heart. Trust. Every moment is an opportunity for rebirth."

– Cheryl Melody Baskin

If You Have a Dream:
A Chakra Guided Visualization

"Hope is the thing with feathers that perches in the soul – and sings the tunes without the words – and never stops at all."

– Emily Dickinson

We are about to use each of the seven chakras to discover and honor all the dreams that live in your heart. To rev up each chakra, we will engage in the world of creative visualization. Visualization, imagination, intuition and creativity are positive energy forces. If you can imagine your dreams in your conscious and subconscious mind, the impossible becomes highly possible.

Implement our "chakra guided visualization" twice. First, focus on a dream you have for yourself. Next, focus on a dream you have for the world. After each visualization exercise, take extra time to process all your dreams, thoughts and feelings by writing them down in an "If You Have a Dream" journal.

Let's begin. Bring your full attention to your *first chakra*. Visualize a healthy "wheel of spinning energy" vibrating and spinning at the base of your spine, soles of your feet, bladder, pelvic floor, and first three vertebrae. Place one hand slightly above the area of your first chakra. Move your hand *counterclockwise* in a circular motion, and at the same time, visualize the power color of *red* surrounding the entire first "wheel of spinning energy." Keep rotating your hand and slowly widen the circle. While doing this, imagine that you are clearing away layers of this chakra that don't serve you well. After a few minutes, stop the motion, rub your hands together, shake off the negative energy, and breathe. Next, smooth the energy of the first chakra by moving your hand *clockwise* this time. Slowly widen the circle. As you breathe into the energy of your first chakra, invite the courage and strength you will need to follow the dreams in your heart. Your root chakra senses your intention and eagerly responds by becoming stronger with every breath. As your first inner vortex becomes increasingly energized, see yourself confidently stepping into your dreams. Sense its energy field pumping through the bottoms of your feet and moving all the way up to the crown of your head. Add positive affirmations to solidify your courage. Here are a few first chakra power words to get you started.

> *"I have the strength, stamina and courage to fuel my dreams."*
> *"I can do this!"*
> *"I am rooted in the earth's grounded energy."*
> *"Courage is part of me."*
> *Strength is part of me."*

As your first chakra expands and flows, focus on your *second chakra*. Your second "wheel of spinning energy" spins above the pubic bone and just below your navel. It is an inner vortex that contains unlimited creative flow. It is also the area of birth and rebirth. Place one of your hands slightly above your second chakra. Move your hand *counterclockwise* in a circular motion, and at the same time, visualize the vibrant color of *orange* surrounding the entire second "wheel of spinning energy." Keep rotating your hand and slowly widen the circle. While doing this, imagine that you are clearing away layers of this chakra that don't serve you well. After a few minutes, stop the motion, rub your hands together, shake off the negative energy, and breathe. Next, smooth the energy of the second chakra by moving your hand *clockwise* this time. Slowly widen the circle as you imagine honoring your second chakra by increasing your level of self-confidence and self-belief. As you encourage this chakra to vibrate to its full capacity, validate yourself. It is your birthright to honor your gifts and your full space in the world. There is no need to play life small, dumb down, berate yourself, or make yourself less than you really are. You are a beautiful child of the universe with many gifts and talents. Step into your innate gifts as if your life depends on it. Believe that every moment is an opportunity to give birth to the passions and dreams that have always lived inside you. Add positive affirmations to solidify the rebirth of creative flow and personal empowerment. Here are a few second chakra power words to get you started.

"I step into all of who I really am."

"I honor my full place in the world."

"I am IN the universe. I am here."

"Every moment is a new opportunity for rebirth."

As the first and second chakras continue to spin vibrantly, invite the *third chakra* to join the party. The third "wheel of spinning energy" vibrates in the solar plexus. This is the energy field of passion, inner fire, light and will. If this inner vortex is weak and the light within you is diminished, do everything you can to reignite your will to live. Believe that you are loved. *You are.* Believe that the world needs your unique gifts. *It does.*

Place one of your hands slightly above your third chakra. Move your hand *counterclockwise* in a circular motion, and at the same time, visualize the beautiful color of *sunshine yellow* surrounding the entire third "wheel of spinning energy." Keep rotating your hand and slowly widen the circle. While doing this, imagine that you are clearing away layers of this chakra that don't serve you well. After a few minutes, stop the motion, rub your hands together, shake off the negative energy, and breathe. Next, smooth the energy of your third chakra by moving your hand *clockwise* this time. Slowly widen the circle as you imagine honoring your third chakra by adding more joy to your life. Add positive affirmations to solidify the fire in your belly and your strong will to live life to the fullest. Here are a few third chakra power words to get you started.

> *"I have the will to live with zest, passion, light and courage."*
>
> *"I am a beacon of light and sparkling energy."*
>
> *"I see life as a wonderous miracle."*
>
> *"I am the spirit of joy."*
>
> *"I am unstoppable!"*

As your first three chakras spin vibrantly, focus on your *fourth chakra*, your heart center. This is the chakra that encourages your heart to open to compassion, forgiveness and love. Place one of your hands slightly above your fourth chakra. Move your hand *counterclockwise* in a circular motion, and at the same time, visualize the soothing color of *emerald green* surrounding your entire fourth "wheel of spinning energy." Keep rotating your hand and slowly widen the circle. While doing this, imagine that you are clearing away layers of this chakra that don't serve you well. After a few minutes, stop the motion, rub your hands together, shake off the negative energy, and breathe. Next, smooth the energy of your fourth chakra by moving your hand *clockwise* this time. Slowly widen the circle as you imagine honoring your fourth chakra by opening yourself to giving and receiving more love. Invite your heart to dance with the spirit of pure love. Step into your dreams and reach out to the world with both arms outstretched wide to the universe. Follow the whispers of your heart. What is your passion? What gives you happiness? What gives you warmth inside your soul? Let the whispers of your heart lead you. They are your guide. Add positive affirmations to solidify the vision of your heart opening to the healing power of love. Here are a few fourth chakra power words to get you started.

"My heart is open to the healing power of love."

"I listen to the whispers of my heart."

"Through love, all things are possible."

"It is safe for me to love and be loved."

As you move to your *fifth chakra,* focus on the area around your throat. This chakra invites you to release your courageous, confident and compassionate voice. It encourages you to reach out to others for support, too. Place one of your hands slightly above your fifth chakra. Move your hand *counterclockwise* in a circular motion, and at the same time, visualize the relaxing color of *sky blue* surrounding your entire fifth "wheel of spinning energy." Keep rotating your hand and slowly widen the circle. While doing this, imagine that you are clearing away layers of this chakra that don't serve you well. After a few minutes, stop the motion, rub your hands together, shake off the negative energy, and breathe. Next, smooth the energy of your fifth chakra by moving your hand *clockwise* this time. Slowly widen the circle and imagine honoring your fifth chakra by giving yourself the freedom to express yourself with more confidence.

When you share your needs and dreams with others, you might be surprised at the quality of support that suddenly surrounds you. The fifth chakra focuses on your ability to voice your truth. It is here that you are brave enough to release your voice and share what you need from others. It is here that you will find a community of like-minded people who will support your dreams. Don't hesitate to ask for what you need in life. *Be* your dreams. Add positive affirmations to honor your birthright to give yourself a voice in the world. Here are a few fifth chakra power words to get you started.

> *"I give myself a clear, compassionate and courageous voice."*
>
> *"I speak my truth with clarity, strength and love."*
>
> *"I matter."*
>
> *"I give myself permission to express my thoughts and feelings. People need to hear from me."*

Focus on your *sixth chakra*. This chakra is also known as your third eye energy center. It is the sacred place of your highest intuition and wisdom. As you place your hand slightly above your forehead and between your two eyebrows, move your hand *counterclockwise* in a circular motion, and at the same time, visualize the strong color of *indigo* surrounding your entire sixth "wheel of spinning energy." Keep rotating your hand and slowly widen the circle. While doing this, imagine that you are clearing away layers of this chakra that don't serve you well. After a few minutes, stop the motion, rub your hands together, shake off the negative energy, and breathe. Next, smooth the energy of your sixth chakra by moving your hand *clockwise* this time. Slowly widen the circle and imagine honoring your sixth chakra by opening yourself to the wisdom of your highest intuition. Ask your third eye ...

> *"What is my highest intuition telling me? What is my innermost truth? What does my heart really want? What are my biggest dreams for myself and what are my biggest dreams for the world? What action steps can I take to make all these dreams come true?"*

Give yourself the breath and the space to hear the answers to all your questions. Even if nothing comes through you right now, trust that the answers are there. Your highest wisdom may come to you in a few hours, in your dreams, tomorrow morning, anytime. Add positive affirmations to help you trust in the unknown. Here are a few sixth chakra power words to get you started.

> *"I give myself the gift of empty space to listen to the whispers of the universe."*
>
> *"I trust in the unknown mysteries of life."*

> *"Something magical is about to happen."*
>
> *"I listen to my highest wisdom."*

The *seventh chakra*, or crown, is the dessert of them all. The Tiramisu of all chakras. The Key Lime pie. Choose any pie at all. The seventh chakra is here to tell you that the universe supports and surrounds you with love, guidance and perfect timing. Place one of your hands slightly above the area of your seventh chakra. Move your hand *counterclockwise* in a circular motion, and at the same time, visualize the healing colors of *violet and white* surrounding your entire seventh "wheel of spinning energy." Keep rotating your hand and slowly widen the circle. While doing this, imagine that you are clearing the layers of this chakra that don't serve you well. After a few minutes, stop the motion, rub your hands together, shake off the negative energy, and breathe. Next, smooth the energy of your seventh chakra by moving your hand *clockwise* this time. Slowly widen the circle and imagine honoring your seventh chakra by trusting in the unknown mystery of life. As this chakra spins, sense your deep connection with the universe as you ask ...

> *"How can I honor all the gifts I've been given?*
> *How can I live a life of loving consciousness?*
> *How can I be a catalyst for peace, justice, love,*
> *unity, positive change and hope?"*

Add positive affirmations to solidify your ability to trust, let go and be at peace. Here are a few seventh chakra power words to get you started.

"I surrender to the natural flow and guidance of the universe."

"I trust."

"I am loved."

"Just for being and breathing, I am enough."

Your seven chakras are now in balance and all the colors merge and swirl up, down and all around your body in a golden coat of protection and love. Anything is possible now - all the dreams you have for yourself and all the dreams you have for the world. Breathe in renewed inner peace, strength, stamina, new dreams, empowerment, confidence, passion, joy, light, love, clarity, freedom, wisdom and trust. Return to the "If You Have a Dream" chakra guided visualization any time you need an extra boost of healing and hope.

One more ingredient - "Sound Healing." If you would like to add even more zing to your chakras, sing an open vowel sound and direct it to one of your chakras. Hold the note as long as you can, take a new breath, and sing the tone again. Sound healing massages your body from inside out and is used as a transformational tool for both in tune *and* out of tune singers. There are no wrong notes. Only the healing power of vibration.

One-of-a-kind. This is one amazing technique, isn't it? Chakra energy balancing clears negative core beliefs, releases emotional toxins, creates physical, emotional and spiritual balance, increases inner peace and happiness, plants the seeds of our dreams deep into our soul, and helps us live with energy, courage, creativity, clarity, strength and flow. Throughout my day, I do a quick body scan and use my intuition to check on the health of each chakra. If I sense that I need a tune-up, I take a few minutes to balance my chakras, and voila! I'm a new person. This technique is one-of-a-kind, and my gratitude for opening my mind and heart to the wonder of this method goes to Energy Medicine expert, Donna Eden (www.innersource.net). She is truly a lightworker.

If we can feel love, peace, hope and healing within ourselves, we can give love, peace, hope and healing to others. It's worth the investment in time to tune your chakras and make yourself glow from inside-out.

A Blueprint for Living Your Dreams

"A leap of faith isn't easy. It takes trust in the
unknown, an open and willing heart, determination,
courage and intuitive wisdom."

— Cheryl Melody Baskin

The seeds for the chakra visualization were inspired by my song,
"If You Have a Dream." It came through me when I was going
through a difficult time. I was down. My energy was low. Out
of the blue, something made me get off the couch and place me
in front of the piano. The rest took care of itself.

*This story is an example of life's mystical
magic. The lyrics that accompany this beautiful melody have helped me time and time
again. The manifestation of this song is another
example that life doesn't have to be perfect to
have something magical and beautiful happen
in your life when you least expect it.*

When I look at these lyrics, I see a blueprint for living my life
as a dreamer and doer. The words guide me in honoring and
manifesting my highest purpose, innate gifts and unstoppable
dreams. Take each word to your heart, peace dreamer. At the
end of the song, you will see positive affirmations. Use these
affirmations as your mantras. They will give you confidence,
determination, faith and trust.

If You Have a Dream

From the albums, *Celebrate!, Listen to the Whispers*
and *Lullabies of Love*

If you have a dream, hold onto the dreamer
Fill yourself up with music and light
Reach out to Spirit who gave you meaning
Trust in your dreams both day and night.

Breathe in who you are
These dreams are not far
And trust in love to guide you
Embrace what you feel you know to be real

Look up high in all you do.

If you have a dream, hold onto the dreamer
Fill yourself up with music and light
Reach out to Spirit who gave you meaning
Trust in your dreams both day and night.

Protect your precious dream
Allow it to be seen
Don't let any darkness surround you
Reach out with both wings, let your heart sing

Look up high in all you do.

If you have a dream, hold onto the dreamer
Fill yourself up with music and light

Reach out to Spirit who gave you meaning
Trust in your dreams both day and night.

Rise to your true self

Your life can be filled with unlimited possibilities

Reach for the stars

You have the power to make your dreams come true

The power is all inside you to dream

To act upon your dreams

To love

To find peace within you

To be all of who you really are

Stand fully in yourself

In your "I AM"

Look up high in all you do.

CHAPTER NINE

Tapping Into the Soul of Peace - Part I

"The structures of your dreamscape have done their work. Far out beyond the bounds of this quiet space where you have built your sanctuary, a larger vision now unfolds. It moves in your thoughts, and surely if it there can find a passage, then likewise must it grow and spread across the mindways of the planet. Its whispers touch the ears of those who listen deeply. Its vistas spread before the eyes of those who look awakened. Its promise reaches out to touch the heart of those who know the purpose for their being."

– Dr. Desmond E. Berghofer

The Visioneers: A Courage Story about Belief in the Future

Stand Proud!

From the album, *Celebrate!*

Stand up, stand up, stand up for yourself
And claim your shining star.
Rise up, rise up, proud of yourself
Please tell us who you are.

All kinds of prejudice came to me
But it won't eat me away.
For with this pain, I have set myself free
And that's who I am today!

We are one family after all
We smile, bleed and breathe the same way.
Red, yellow, black or white, short or tall
Stand proud, stand proud today.

Stand up, stand up, stand up for yourself
You are beautiful as can be.
Rise up, rise up, proud of yourself
And set our one family free!

Peace From Inside-Out and Outside-In

"I dwell in possibility."

– Emily Dickinson

Like Emily Dickinson, I believe in possibility, too. The possibility that one day I will feel more peace in my soul, the hope that you will feel more peace in yours, and the possibility of manifesting more peace in the soul of the world. I want nothing more than to change the consciousness of humanity and create a world of love. I want nothing more than to bring people together. I have another intention, too, and it is perhaps the most challenging work of all. What do I need to do first, last and in-between? "Clean my own house." Perhaps you are familiar with this metaphor, too. "Cleaning our own house" is the most complicated "peace begins with me" task of all. It takes courage, humility, inner work, facing our fears, and doing our best to heal some of our history. It isn't easy, and in fact, it may not be possible to heal every relationship from the past and in the present. Everyone involved would need to have the same desire and courage. We can only change what we can change. "The Serenity Prayer," written by American theologian, Reinhold Niebuhr, says it best. "God grant me the serenity to accept the things I cannot change, the courage to change the things I can, and the wisdom to know the difference."

It is exciting to work for causes that can heal the world, and it is equally as exciting to grow from inside-out, transform, question ourselves from within, and shift. We are not what we do. Not our professions, labels or college degrees. We are imperfect human beings, and as my mother used to say, "everyone puts one pant leg on at a time." No one is immune from looking within. As you go through your day, witness yourself. What needs repair? Were your thoughts and words helpful today? Did they tear someone down, or did they raise them up? Did your actions and reactions come from the highest place within you? Let's do our best to walk our talk in every part of our lives. If we judged too many times, yelled too many times, felt impatient and angry ...

Stop. Listen. Witness. Forgive yourself. Shift your heart to love. Try again.

It's hard work to clean our own house, both literally and metaphorically. There are emotional triggers, painful history, open wounds and deep scars. But to *be* the peace and to *be* the love we yearn for in the world, examining our lives is soul-cleansing. It is humbling to realize that there is still room for us to grow from inside-out. *Being* peace requires inner inquiry, heightened mindfulness, self-love, kindness, compassion, forgiveness and empathy.

Sadly, you may have encountered peace leaders or wise gurus who didn't do their best to "walk their talk." After all, they are human, too. They have their own inner work to do. It is not okay to abuse someone in your home or at work and then stand in front of thousands of people and preach love and peace. Nothing is more important than living the phrase, "peace begins with me." Will I fall short? Yes. Time and time again. Will you? Yes. Time and time again. We are human. Does it mean we should give up? Never.

To clean my own house, I often ask myself, "How many biases have I stored internally without realizing it? Do I really want to be the kind of person who judges, stereotypes and profiles people who are different from me? Are all my actions, words, feelings and thoughts congruent with my core value of love? How can I learn to *be* the peace and *be* the love I envision for the world?"

Many of us do our best to be good people. We have generous hearts, are kind and caring, resolve conflicts peacefully, and work hard to brainstorm loving ways to heal broken relationships. We do everything we can to heal ourselves. We do everything we can to shift the world towards love. Most of all, we have the sincere intention of being a better person today than we were yesterday.

True activism begins in our core. Our soul of souls.
True activism begins from inside-out.

The W-A-F-T Approach to Peace and Love

> "If you could only sense how important you are
> to the lives of those you meet; how important you
> can be to people that you never dreamed of. There
> is something of yourself that you leave at every
> meeting with another person."
>
> **— Fred Rogers**

For many years, I taught a creative arts program called, "Peace Begins with Me." The curriculum consisted of meaningful music, message-based stories, large multicultural puppets, unique instruments, and most of all, important life lessons. To help my students remember how to look within themselves to determine if they were the peace they wanted in the world, I developed the W-A-F-T method. It was a catchy way for them to remember the importance of their "**W**ords, **A**ctions, **F**eelings and **T**houghts. I made it into a fun snapping and clapping group rap, and when we finished, we would talk about all the deeper messages. It helped my students reflect on whether their words, actions, feelings and thoughts mirrored the vibration of love and peace or whether they needed to tweak them a little.

This approach provided opportunities for greater mindfulness in my own life, too. It is a checklist that heightens personal awareness. As you reflect on your day, ask yourself ...

W: Words

Conscious Communication. What words did I say today and in what tone of voice did I say them? Did I put myself down, or did I empower myself with confidence, love and strength? What words did I say to someone else and in what tone of voice did I say them? Did I put someone down and demean them? Did I listen to their feelings and support them? Did my words mirror agitation, control, judgment and criticism, or did my words embody empathy, forgiveness and love?

A: Actions

Conscious Actions and Reactions. Was I mindful of my actions and reactions today? Did I show love, shine love and stand for love? Did I include people who were different from me? Did I listen to their point of view? Did I say "please" and "thank you?" Open the door for someone? Help someone in need? Apologize when I hurt someone's feelings? Hear someone's life story? Offer my time to help a worthy cause? When I didn't agree with someone, did I try to find common ground? Was I mindful of my own biases? What action did I take?

F: Feelings

Conscious Feelings. There is an ebb and flow to feelings. What are you feeling about the state of our world? Our government? Family? Friends? People who don't agree with you and people who do? What are you feeling about yourself and your life? If you're sad, angry or confused, acknowledge your feelings. Life isn't easy, I know. Is there anything you might be willing to do to shift your mood? How about positive distraction? Try laughter, movement, the creative arts, journal writing, nature walks, music, and using your imagination to visualize a better picture for your life. Any of these choices will shift your attention towards light and hope. If you can see it in your imagination, it will be so. If you can feel it in your heart, it will be so.

T: Thoughts

Conscious Thoughts. Mindfulness meditation experts call our minds, "monkey minds." Our minds flit from one distraction to another, often spending time making unfair judgments. If you are deep in a whirlwind of negativity, stop yourself from judging yourself and others. Everyone's heart beats in the same way, pain is the same, and wanting love is the same. Listen to each person's story of challenge, personal growth and triumph and shift to thoughts of love, peaceful conflict-resolution, compromise and optimism.

> *With the W-A-F-T method, we will have both good days and bad. That's the joy of waking up to a new day. It's a new beginning. Above all, thank you for being open to the W-A-F-T approach, for listening to the whispers of the good within your own soul, and for doing everything you can to project the essence of peace, love and hope.*

Full Circle

"Strength does not come from physical capacity. It comes from an indomitable will."

– Mahatma Gandhi

I was doing my best to organize all the papers flying around in one of my big messy drawers. After an hour, (*I told you it was a big messy drawer*), I stumbled upon a treasure. It was a crinkled-up paper that had a vaguely familiar poem on it. The title gave me goosebumps. I had written a version of one of my "Shift of Heart" poems when I was only fifteen. I guess I have always envisioned a world that was filled with peace, unity and love. Even at a young age, I felt strongly that anyone - even someone who chose violence, discrimination and hatred as their path - had the power to shift their heart towards love.

When I think back, my views about peace formed when I was even younger than fifteen. In fact, I was only five. That was the age when I experienced endless teasing, bullying and religious persecution. I remember feeling confused. I couldn't understand why I was called names and physically assaulted for belonging to a minority religion. I was innocent and loving. All I wanted was a world that embraced the values of tolerance, acceptance, inclusion and respect.

As I held the poem in my hands, I could feel the essence of my soul at five and fifteen come full circle with the person I am now at seventy. Innately and innocently, I have always believed in a world of equality, unity, justice, kindness, empathy, love, peace and hope. I will continue to do so until my last breath.

My Dream for Peace

"Join me as I imagine, believe, dream, trust, hope, envision, rejoice, visualize and celebrate the healing energy of peace, unity, justice and love."

– Cheryl Melody Baskin

"Shift of Heart"

Imagine: A day will come when those who have the power to destroy the world suddenly feel a transformational shift in their hearts to save the world.

Believe: A day will come when every heart on earth opens to the healing energy of love, kindness, compassion, empathy, diversity celebration and peace.

Dream: A day will come when no one is ever judged again based on their color, race, religion, creed, nationality, gender, age, ability, social status or sexual orientation.

Trust: A day will come when we see each other through the warm eyes of love.

Rejoice: A day will come when the Statue of Liberty stands tall once again and greets all humanity back to its shores with love.

Envision: A day will come when the world chooses to cooperate, collaborate, and do what is best for the well-being of the collective whole.

Care: A day will come when we realize how important it is to stop our busy lives and listen to each other's feelings, thoughts and life experiences without judgment. We will simply listen from a place of love.

Visualize: A day will come when conflicts are resolved through nonviolent solutions, empathic listening, common ground compromise, and the healing power of love.

Celebrate: A day will come when a healing light shines through and around mother earth and the whole world makes a conscious decision to stand for love, unity, justice, equality and peace.

An Invitation

"You are loved just for being who you are, just for existing. You don't have to do anything to earn it. Your shortcomings, your lack of self-esteem, physical perfection, or social and economic success - none of it matters. No one can take this love away from you and it will always be here."

– Ram Dass

I chose a life of high visibility on Facebook for a reason. With unconditional love, inclusion, kindness and compassion as the focus, my mission is to bring people together. As the founder, moderator and intuitive life coach of the *Shift of Heart* community, it is an honor to create a place of peace for anyone who yearns to be accepted and loved. Together, we have made deep connections with strangers who have become our friends. When someone joins, they are welcomed. When someone is ill, we form a circle of light, love and healing around them. Because people feel safe in this confidential community, they are free to be themselves and share what is in their hearts. Our conversations are sometimes deep and sometimes light, but the common threads that run through every discussion are compassion, empathy, support, inner inquiry, gratefulness, positivity, wisdom, inclusion, hope, peace, love, and caring about the collective whole. Everyone needs to feel loved, seen, accepted, included, heard and valued, and *Shift of Heart* is answering this need. On any given day, I might offer a positive affirmation and ask the group for feedback, share a personal philosophy, post an uplifting song, add a life coaching video, create an open-ended question, or reflect on one of the member's thoughts or affirmations.

Shift of Heart is based on the following mission statement ...

> *"Shift of Heart" is a microcosm of everything good that is possible for our world. Together, we have the collective intention of becoming a global community of inclusion, positivity, healing, inspiration, dreams, compassion, heart, empathy, support, wisdom and light. Most of all, we are here to help each other breathe in the positive vibrations of peace, love and hope. Here you will find open hearts. Manners. Welcoming. Inclusion. Respect. An island of peace. Acceptance. Love.*

The following sections contain brief *Shift of Heart* excerpts. Each discussion includes intuitive life coaching, inner inquiry, and community interaction ...

Life Coach (me) - "Hundreds of our *Shift of Heart* members shared their power words a few weeks ago. Let's revisit this idea. Words matter."

➤ *Power words shared by members of the "Shift of Heart" community ...*

Determination, strength, peace, relief, faith, happiness, positivity, awareness, commitment, heart, self-care, breath, hope, persistence, gratefulness, acceptance, selfless service, daily recreation, cherish, connection, solitude, nourishment, silence, love, protection, nature, quietude, mindfulness, confidence, renewal, begin again, open heart, support, kindness, compassion, empathy, self-worth, creativity, family, restoration, harmony, balance, focus, staying calm, honor, integrity, nobility, humility, evolution, fellowship, namaste, understanding, loving-kindness, courage, clarity, fortitude, equality, open-minded, respect, listening to my inner voice, intuition, imagination, self-love, activism, healing, happy, introspective, united, grace, tenderness, "be," light, awakening, reverence, fearless, shift, Gaia, appreciation, fun, constancy, rejuvenate, resilience, wisdom, illuminate, laughter, reemerge, optimistic, radiant, patience, inner peace, dignity, forgiveness, freedom, health, restart.

- *To my reader - What are your favorite power words?*

Life Coach: "Every moment is an opportunity for rebirth and to try again. What gift will you give yourself today?"

➢ *Wisdom shared by members of the "Shift of Heart" community ...*

- I will pace myself today.

- I will be patient with myself.

- I will offer myself love and understanding,

- I will offer myself forgiveness.

- I will play in my tiny indoor garden, reading a good mystery book and cooking myself a yummy healthy dinner.

- I will release the need to work on every bit of information I take in. I will let go of things I can't control, let them be what they are, realizing I'm not responsible for everything in the world.

- I am aiming for freedom from stress.

- Laughter.

- Patience.

- Love.

- I will observe without thinking or judging.

- Courage and letting go.

- I will give myself the freedom from perfectionism that wastes time and energy. I will spend time taking care of myself.

- Rest and peace.

- Kindness and self-love.

- Perseverance. I will not give up.

- *To my reader – What gift will you give yourself today?*

Life Coach: "Today, when you take part in a conversation, simply listen to the other person for awhile. Listen with your heart. Instead of reacting right away, just allow that person the space and time to be heard without judgment. Notice if the "listening with your heart" process created a positive outcome in any way."

➤ *Wisdom shared by several members of the "Shift of Heart" community ...*

- This literally happened to me yesterday. I received a phone call from someone who was terribly upset and just needed someone to listen to them. Gradually they calmed down and the conversation ended well. The power of listening and being listened to is a major lesson.

- Thank you, Melody. I shared a post that expressed my opinion. One of the comments got ugly, but I followed your advice and stay centered and loving.

Life Coach: "There is a champion inside you. Tell us what you do, say or think to make this affirmation true in your life."

➤ *Wisdom shared by members of the "Shift of Heart" community ...*

- I show patience and perseverance.

- I care and believe in myself.

- I have faith in God and belief in the value of all humans.

- After losing my husband to Lewy Body Dementia in my early 60s after years of caregiving, I made a conscious decision to become my own person once again. It was and is important to me not to be defined by my heartache, but to step beyond grief and give generously of my time with a joyful heart, sing unabashedly, spend time with kids, and take care of myself.

- I am persistent and determined. I rarely, if ever, give up.

- Faith. Letting go of people who truly don't care.

- *To my reader – I know there's a champion inside you, too. Please write and share your own story of determination, resilience and strength.*

September 18, 2020 - Remembering Justice Ruth Bader Ginsberg

Life Coach: "Equality, justice, courage, nobility, dignity, stamina, persistence, resilience, heart, focus, trust, humor, strength, brilliance. Ruth Bader Ginsberg embodies each quality." Patricia added, "She was an incredible warrior, change catalyst and truth-exposing woman." Sue added, "She was a light in the darkness." I added, "Let's look at what Ruth Bader Ginsberg symbolized and become it."

Life Coach: "Have you received an act of kindness or offered one? No matter how little or big, it counts! It changes the energy frequency of the planet into a higher vibration. Let's bring light and hope to others by documenting quick stories and examples. Sending each of you the love and the kindness you so richly deserve."

➤ *Acts of kindness shared by members of the "Shift of Heart" community ...*

- I was called to a friend's condo yesterday. She needed a handlebar put up so she could safely get out of her shower. So, I got my tools and installed it. She was so happy. She asked me how much she owed me, and I said, "Your loving energy sent to me when you think of it." She laughed! I love helping people love where they live!

- I was cleaning up my house this weekend and decided to take some things to Goodwill. But I kept thinking about a young single mom I know. I texted her and learned she was just researching the very item I offered her!

- Five special women got together to celebrate my birthday on Friday. We met at the restaurant, they brought balloons, cupcakes, gifts – even though I requested no gifts – it really made me feel special. I told each one of them how special they are to me and how each one brings the unique gift of themselves to me. I'd been down, but these wonderful women friends elevated me to the point that I'm seeing beauty again. Thank you for this important reminder – to be aware of acts of kindness.

- I helped a friend with her new apartment. I try to be a giver and not to expect anything in return. Just the gratitude in doing something for someone else.

- *To my reader – Have you received an act of kindness or offered one?*

November 3, 2020 - The Presidential Election

Life Coach: "Dear *Shift of Heart* community, I know it's election day. Whatever the outcome, shine love, be love and stand for love. Focus on being and spreading peace. Be grateful for all the abundance around you. Do good things. Breathe in joy."

November 4, 2020 - Waiting for the results

Life Coach: "Be gentle with yourself, today. It doesn't matter what anyone else does. It only matters how we conduct our own lives. Integrity, truth, kindness, grace, compassion, empathy, forgiveness, love. That's what matters. Stay calm. Let nature heal you. Breathe. Instead of thinking negatively, think of what is possible for yourself and for the world."

November 7, 2020 - The election results

Life Coach: "The United States elected a new president and vice-president. May Joe Biden and Kamala Harris help us through to the other side of division, upheaval and chaos towards unity, justice, light, healing, peace and love."

Life Coach: "Despite what is going on nationally, globally or personally, stay focused on the *good* in life. On kindness, love, compassion, empathy, peace, hope, caring, faith, music that uplifts your spirit and calms your soul, optimism and light. Take healing walks in nature, sing to the birds, hum a little hum as

Winnie-the-Pooh says, and focus on the quality of gratefulness. When you feel anxious, return to your breath and this moment. Offer nurturing acts of kindness to yourself. Offer nurturing acts of kindness to others. Keep your body, mind and spirit as balanced as possible."

I have loved sharing the magnificence of this community with you. Thanks to the magic of technology, we can connect with people from all over the world. It is gratifying to read each other's words of wisdom and support, and I'm sure your wisdom and support would be appreciated by our "Shift of Heart" community, too. Come join us for a boost of positivity and light. We would love to have you!

https://www.facebook.com/groups/103850356767217/

Healing the World Through Love

"Listen to the wind. It talks. Listen to the silence. It speaks. Listen to your heart. It knows."

– Native American Proverb

People are anxious. Anxious about the political beliefs of others, anxious about COVID-19, anxious about their lives after COVID-19, anxious about the economy, anxious about racism, anxious about their rights, anxious about everything. It may or may not be true, but it feels as if democracy, justice, unity, compassion, nonviolent conflict-resolution, earth preservation, respect, kindness, caring and peace are all on the line.

In my heart of hearts, I know that our best nature will shine through the darkness. One peace dreamer at a time, we will change the world. Together, we will heal it through love. We will also heal our divisions and prejudices by shifting our minds and hearts to a new story of human consciousness. It is possible.

How do I know? Take our highly polarized presidential election as an example. The determination that people of *all* political beliefs exemplified during the presidential election was amazing to witness. Americans voted in record numbers. In the heat. In the cold. All ages. As old as 109. All colors, races, religions, genders, nationalities. During a pandemic. Imagine! Even during a pandemic, people wanted their voices heard and they risked their lives to vote. They drove for miles, stood in line for hours, brought a bag lunch, brought a chair, sang, talked, danced, stayed physically distanced and wore face masks. No attempt at voter suppression deterred anyone. They would find a way to exercise their right to vote, no matter what. They stepped up with stoic determination, will, resilience, courage, strength, individuality, passion and persistence. Nothing could stop people from doing what they felt was important to their freedom, survival and rights as a citizen.

> *If the values of respect, kindness, inclusion and unconditional love could merge with the amazing determination I witnessed on that day, the world would have it made. Love, peace, transformation, possibility and hope are always on the grand stage of life smiling, waving us on, and standing by.*

CHAPTER TEN

Tapping Into the Soul of Peace - Part II

"Nothing reduces prejudice and racism more than having the courage to forge friendships with those considered different than yourself."

– Arthur P. Ciaramicoli, Ed.D., Ph.D.

The Triumph of Diversity: Rejoice in and Benefit from the Interconnectedness of Humankind

We are Always at the Beginning

"Pursue some path, however narrow and crooked, in
which you can walk with love and reverence."

— Henry David Thoreau

Dearest Peace Dreamer,

We are always at the beginning when it comes to learning about
our own biases. We are always at the beginning when it comes
to healing the injustices of the world. By now, you know what
I'm going to say to you. *Never give up.*

Keep looking within, ask soul-searching questions, heal yourself,
work on healing the relationships in your life, and continue to
help our planet any way you envision best.

Step boldly into being a positive energy force for the world.
All paths that embody peace and love ignite possibility, light,
promise and hope in ourselves and in others. Always know in
your heart that peace is possible.

It only takes one person to propel the dream for a kinder and
more inclusive world. Because of you, every positive vision
becomes possible. Even love. *Especially* love. Even peace.
Especially peace.

Anything we can do to advocate for equality, inclusion, respect, justice and compassion will leave a lasting imprint that ultimately influences the positive actions of many.

Wisdom From a Peace Dreamer

"There is no remedy for love but to love more."

— Henry David Thoreau

The path to raising consciousness includes the constant process of looking within, adjusting our own behavior, and simultaneously working on transforming the wounds of the world to a place of love. I leave you with a little more *Peace Dreamer* wisdom to breathe into your soul ...

- Nurture yourself to nurture others. Peace work takes stamina. Take care of yourself.

- Immerse yourself in nature as often as possible. It is always here to nurture you back to physical, emotional, mental and spiritual health.

- Revere the earth. Take care of it.

- Revere all people. Respect them.

- Whatever path someone has chosen, send them your light, love and healing.

- Racism and other prejudices are ingrained and learned across generations, but changes in human consciousness are always possible at any given moment. Everyone has the power to shift, grow and transform.

- We have the potential to be so much more than just a face and a voice to each other. We are a name, pulse, person and life story waiting to be known.

- Keep your heart wide open.

- Whenever possible, make your decisions based on the greater good of the collective whole.

- Listen to life's wisdom whispers.

- Keep your seven chakras tuned to their highest vibrations.

- Be patient with the process of personal growth and transformation.

- Use positive affirmations throughout your day.

- Be curious about people. Honor everyone's life story.

- Trust in the ebb and flow of your life.

- Leave time to daydream.

- Never give up or think it's too late to grow, learn and love.

- Forgive yourself. Let go of shame, regret and guilt. Every day is an opportunity for a new beginning.

- Forgive others.

- Stay determined, resilient and strong.

- Allow yourself to be heard and seen. Believe in yourself. You were given unique gifts for a reason. Don't shrivel yourself up and make yourself small.

- Shine your light. Become the heart of peace. Do your part to bring more love into the world.

- Create. It's healing to the soul.

- Flow with the magical mystery of the unknown.

- Embody the spirit of the butterfly. Change, growth and transformation are possible at any moment.

- Be an unstoppable peace dreamer. Soar!

- No matter what, keep walking the path of peace, love, dreams, miracles and magic.

- Practice the art of mindfulness in determining the quality of your words, thoughts, feelings, actions and reactions. Are they giving you the gift of inner peace and love? Are they giving those around you the gift of peace and love?

- Envision a world that rejoices in its diversity.

- Spread love, peace and hope wherever you go.

A Circle of Peace, Love and Hope

"When you find just the right place and just the
right fit for your passions and dreams,
your heart will sing forever."

– Cheryl Melody Baskin

The following list isn't just a long boring roster of names. The list is here to inspire us. It is filled with ordinary people who followed their extraordinary dreams. Each person stands for peace, justice, unity, positive change, hope and love. When I look at all these names, I can feel each person's courage, energy, passion and dreams. When I look at all these names, it makes me want to be a better person and do my part to help create a world of love and peace, too. As you look at this list, feel the positive vibrations of each lightworker, visionary, healer, changemaker and peacebuilder. Breathe their energy and vision into your soul and let their passions ignite yours.

Ordinary People with Extraordinary Dreams

Justice Ruth Bader Ginsberg; Rosa Parks; Martin Luther King, Jr.; Mahatma Gandhi; Harriet Tubman; Nelson Mandela; Desmond

Tutu; United Nations former Assistant Secretary-General, Dr. Robert Muller, (www.robertmuller.org); Barbara Gaughen-Muller, President of the United Nations Association - Santa Barbara, (www.unasb.org), President of the Rotary E-Club of World Peace, (www.rotaryeclubofworldpeace.org); Dr. Desmond Berghofer, The Visioneers International Network, (www.thevisioneers.ca); Dr. Geraldine Schwartz, The Visioneers International Network, (www.thevisioneers.ca); United Nations Ambassador, Anwarul K. Chowdbury; Anne Frank; Elie Wiesel; Representative John Lewis; Representative Elijah Cummings; Senator John McCain, (www.mccaininstitute.org); Alan O'Hare; Bernie S. Siegel, M.D., (www.berniesiegelmd.com); Kristin Hoffmann, (www.kristinhoffmann.com); Arthur P. Ciaramicoli, Ed.D., Ph.D., (www.balanceyoursuccess.com); Liseli A. Fitzpatrick, Ph.D., (https://www.wellesley.edu/africana/faculty/fitzpatrick); LeBron James, (www.lebronjames.com); Mother Teresa; Reverend Dr. Deborah L. Clark, (www.openspiritcenter.org); Mattie Stepanek, (www.mattieonline.com); Peace Pilgrim, (www.peacepilgrim.org); Philip M. Hellmich, (www.theshiftnetwork.com); Heart Phoenix, (www.centerforpeacebuilding.org); Liz Gannon Graydon, (www.peacealliance.org); Jelena Popovic, (www.peacealliance.org); Terry Mason, (www.peacealliance.org); The Honorable Douglas Roche; Environmental activist, Greta Thunberg; Rotary Action Group for Peace, Dennis Wong; Founder of the Green Hope Foundation and child rights activist, Kehkashan Basu; James Barez, (www.awakeningjoy.com); Founder of Garden of Light, Reverend Deborah Maldow, (www.revdeborah.com); United Nations Youth Delegate to Pathways to Peace, Betsabe Reyna; Founder of the Global Movement for the Culture of Peace, Iris Spellings; Pakistani activist for female education and Nobel Prize laureate, Malala Yousafzai; Nina Meyerhof, (www.coeworld.org); Rachel Maddow, (www.rachelmaddow.com); Dot Maver, (www.

nationalpeaceacademy.us); Anne Baring, Ph.D., (www.annebaring. com); Tatiana Speed, (www.thevisioneers.ca); United Nations Humanitarian Artist, Ricky Kej, (www.rickykej.com); Kareem Abdul-Jabbar, (www.kareemabduljabbar.com); Aaron Friedland, (www.thevisioneers.ca); Cyril Richie, (www.thevisioneers.ca); Jan Krause Greene, (www.jkgreene.com); Ukpeme Okon, (www. thevisioneers.ca); Cynthia Franca, (www.thevisioneers.ca), Dorothy Walsh, (www.thevisioneers.ca); Elizabeth Gilbert, (www. elizabethgilbert.com); Rob Bell, (www.robbell.com); all members of the *Shift of Heart* Facebook Community; Dr. Norma J. Leslie; Bob Silverstein; Elisa Pearmain, (www.elisapearmain.com); Joyce Wycoff, (www.joycewycoff.com); Susan Perry; Virginia Swain; Wendy Young; Judes Look-Why; Irene Hannigan; Ann Marie Speicher; Barry Rosenbloom; Heidi Hackett; Sonja Dahlgren; Shelley Phillips; Michaelene Morris; Deborah Burke Henderson; Ronda Lanzetta; Mary E. Mitchell, (www.marymitchell.com); Sister Denise Kelly, CSJ; Len and Libby Traubman; Dr. Kathleen O'Malley, (www.thevisioneers.ca); Sister Ellie Daniels, CSJ; Lynn Hopkins Watson; Janet Rose Ferreri; Michelle Obama; President Barack Obama, (www.barackobama.com); President Jimmy Carter, (www.cartercenter.org); Oprah Winfrey, (www.oprah. com); all members of the Visioneers International Network, (www.thevisioneers.ca) ...

And there are many other names that belong in this circle of peace, love and hope. For example, yours. Thank you for doing your part to help make this world a kinder and more inclusive place in which to live.

Words to Live By

"I know nothing in the world that has as much power as a word. Sometimes I write one, and I look at it, until it begins to shine."

– Emily Dickinson

Emily Dickinson was right. "There is nothing in the world that has as much power as a word." Here are some of the highlights from *Peace Dreamer*. Each word represents my highest wisdom, open heart and starry-eyed dreams.

Power Quotes from *Peace Dreamer*

True activism begins in our core. Our soul of souls. True activism begins from inside-out.

What happened in the past is what happened in the past. You have the power to define who you are now. Every moment is a new beginning. Make it count.

As we work on resolving the many injustices that plague our planet, it is equally important to focus on healing the wounds that are in our own soul, too. The phrase, "peace begins with me," rings true. The process towards inner healing and healing our planet are connected. It is important to do everything we can to create an alignment between both worlds.

Question to self: How can I let go of my inner judge and shift my heart from fear and judgment to compassion, empathy and love?

Look within. The answers that you are seeking from someone else are all inside you. You are your own inner guru and guide. Listen to the wisdom whispers of the universe. Follow your heart, highest wisdom, intuition, and inner voice. Listen.

Anything we can do to advocate for equality, inclusion, respect, justice, and compassion will leave a lasting imprint that ultimately influences the positive actions of many.

How can we honor the gifts we've been given? What can we do to live a life of loving consciousness? How can we be a catalyst for peace, justice, love, unity, positive change and hope?

Let's embrace the healing power of the collective whole and envision what we could accomplish if we were willing to see each other through the eyes of joy and love.

Racial injustice - or any kind of injustice - is about all of us. Everyone is accountable for each word, action, reaction, feeling and thought rooted in prejudice.

———————————————

Anyone who is courageous enough to take a hard and honest look at themselves can make a conscious and life-changing decision to shift their mindset to one of inclusion, respect and empathy. It is never too late. We have the power to change the way we react to each other. We have the power to shift our hearts towards love.

———————————————

Although it is much more difficult to send love, light and healing to those who have chosen violence, discrimination, bullying, fear and hatred as a way of life, it is important to remember that every human being from every walk of life needs an aura of love, light and healing. You never know. They may sense our "Metta Meditation Prayer of Loving-Kindness" through thought transference and be changed by it.

———————————————

Are all my actions, reactions, words, feelings and thoughts aligned with my core value of love?

———————————————

Stop. Listen. Witness. Forgive yourself. Shift your heart to love. Try again.

———————————————

Every positive action that shines love and stands for love is all that is needed to create a compassionate and inclusive world. The time is now to elevate humanity to a new awakening.

Be a lightworker amid the darkness.

"Keep faith in the goodness of people," the wisdom whisper said. "Don't lose hope. Set an example. Be a role model. Find a way to show the world how to be love. Choose work that will make a difference in the consciousness of others."

We never know, at any moment, who will be the teacher and who will be the student.

To BE the peace and to BE the love we yearn for in the world, examining our lives is soul-cleansing. It is a humbling experience to realize that there is still room for us to grow from inside-out. Being peace requires inner inquiry, humility, mindfulness, love, kindness, compassion, forgiveness and empathy.

I can handle this situation. Step by step and breath by breath, I have the strength to deal with anything that comes my way. I've proven my inner strength before, and I will prove it again. I can do this!

We have the power to change the way we react to each other. We have the power to shift our hearts to love.

Is this thought a weed that needs to be discarded, released and pulled out from its root, or is it a sunflower gradually unfolding into its full potential? If we are mostly critical, snarly, and "glass half empty" thinkers, it would be beneficial to shift our disgruntled attitude as quickly as possible. After all, too many weeds in our garden of life will keep the sunlight from shining and our life from blossoming into its full potential.

Let's acknowledge our imperfections, and at the same time, let's also acknowledge our authentic intention to co-create one humanity of love, inclusion and peace.

Everyone's heart beats in the same way, pain is the same, and wanting love is the same. Listen to each person's story of challenge, personal growth and triumph and shift to thoughts of love, peaceful conflict-resolution, compromise and optimism.

Step boldly into being a positive energy force. All paths that embody peace and love ignite possibility, light, promise and hope in ourselves and in others.

You never know what can happen if you open your heart to the unknown mysteries of life.

Every issue is important and every injustice is unacceptable. Let's do our part to help make this world a more loving and compassionate place. There is no time to lose.

You are enough just for being, breathing, and trying to do better than yesterday. Acknowledge yourself and say, "I am enough."

Ask a higher consciousness from within to guide you.

Don't withdraw or give into your fears. Step into your full potential, stay strong, and find positive ways to serve as a beacon of light and hope to others.

Gratefulness feeds our spirit and reminds us that the greatest joys in life are often found in the simple things.

When someone is upset with you, remember that there are often deep wounds that stir inside their soul that have nothing at all to do with you.

When we use peace as a verb, its meaning is simple. Kindness, compassion, forgiveness, an open heart, an open mind, self-reflection, empathy, helping each other in times of need, a warm smile, manners, and an intention of the heart and to the heart to reach beyond all borders and differences.

If you want to change your life, change your words. Power words shift the trajectory of our lives.

If you can see it in your imagination, it will be so. If you can feel it in your heart, it will be so.

Never give up on yourself and never give up on your dreams for a better world. When you least expect it, your life will shift. You will experience light on your face and hope in your heart. Trust. Every moment is an opportunity for rebirth.

Despite all the chaos, point your North Star towards peace, love, justice, unity, forgiveness, integrity, empathy, truth, kindness, compassion and hope. We can only control what we can control. Stay the course. Know that you are making a positive difference.

Reaffirm your focused archer-with-a-bow dreams and continue to work tirelessly towards a world in which we can all be proud. Never give up. Focus on values that elevate and uplift the human soul and embrace the essence of love.

Love, peace, transformation, possibility and hope are always on the grand stage of life smiling, waving us on, and standing by.

If we make a choice to embody the spirit of loving consciousness, we will be able to shift our hearts from fear to love and honor the most authentic definition of "peace begins with me." The only way we can surround the planet with an inclusive vibration of peace is if we surround the planet with an inclusive vibration of love.

The dream for inner peace and peace in our world begins as a thought, a small seed, an intention, a hope, and a small or big action step. The longing stirs inside the heart of every peace dreamer. The dream begins with me. The dream begins with you.

Keep your heart open and your eyes up towards the light of hope. It is never too late to notice the silver lining from difficult experiences. It is never too late to step into a new purpose, mission and dream for yourself and for the world.

Follow Your Heart

From the album, *Listen to the Whispers,* and the book,
*Heart-Dreamer: Stepping into Life, Love, Creativity
and Dreams - No Matter What*

*"Follow Your Heart" is a guide for all
dreamers and doers ...*

It's a simple song of living
I know just what to do
Follow your heart, let it lead you

Let your heart be your guide every single day
Let it shine a light toward love all along your way.

Follow your bliss, follow your light
What do you want? It will be alright.

Look for the warmth that you feel inside
Follow the joy with your heart open wide.

What is your passion? What feels so good?
Don't live your life with wish and should

Follow the path that's unique to you
Follow your heart in what you feel and do.

It's a simple song of living
I know just what to do
Follow your heart, let it lead you

Let your heart be your guide every single day
Let it shine a light toward hope all along your way.

Special Acknowledgments

Dr. Desmond E. Berghofer (contributor) - Thank you for your extraordinary ability to envision a new story of hope for the world in your powerful book, *The Visioneers: A Courage Story about Belief in the Future*. Every project that you have created has the future of peace and sustainability in your brilliant mind and open heart. In addition to being an extremely powerful writer, you have been an educator; consultant on leadership and the creative management of change; Assistant Deputy Minister of Advanced Education with the Government of Alberta; represented Canada internationally through the Council of Ministers of Education, Canada and the United Nations Educational, Scientific and Cultural Organization (UNESCO); produced and directed a groundbreaking film, *When the Earth Still had 1000 Days*, which featured the inspirational message of Dr. Robert Muller to the Global Citizenship Youth Congress in Vancouver, Canada. You also established The Institute for Ethical Leadership, www.ethicalleadership.com, Grandparents for the Future, co-founded The Visioneers International Network, www.thevisioneers.ca. One person's passion. Yours, Desmond. Thank you for all you do to bring so much good into our world.

Dr. Geraldine Schwartz (contributor) - As a teacher, guidance counselor, neuroscientist, applied clinical psychologist, researcher, founder of The Vancouver Learning Center and co-founder of The Visioneers International Network Web of Good Work and Virtual Expo, there is no limit within you for creating an idea that never existed before. As several of your original poems echo, "YES!" You have said YES to dreams, life, new visions and to peace. You and Desmond are shining examples of the power of love and what can be possible when you put all your dreams into action. Thank you, Gerri, for your friendship, determination, imagination, vision, energy, thought, heart and inspiration. www.thevisioneers.ca

Dr. Robert Muller (contributor) - If you want to know about an amazing peacebuilder, please read all the information and books you can on Dr. Robert Muller, www.robertmuller.org. It would take another book to mention everything this one human being has done for our world in his 88 years on earth. He is the former United Nations Assistant Secretary-General and is instrumental in the conception of many multilateral bodies, including the World Food Program, the United Nations Population Fund and the World Youth Assembly. He also created the *World Core Curriculum* which earned him the United Nations Educational, Scientific and Cultural Organization Prize for Peace Education (UNESCO). Many additional awards have been bestowed on this great man of peace, including the Albert Schweitzer International Prize for the Humanities and the Eleanor Roosevelt Man of Vision Award. He was also nominated 23 times for the Nobel Peace Prize. And what a prolific author! At least fourteen books. Sitting on my desk right now is *Most of All They Taught Me Happiness*. He also co-wrote a daily email newsletter called, *7500 Ideas and Dreams for a Better World,* www.GoodMorningWorld.org. One person with a dream for peace. That's all it takes.

Barbara Gaughen-Muller (contributor and testimonial) - How can one person do all this? You continued Dr. Robert Muller's amazing work as a peacebuilder; became a peace scholar yourself; created Gaughen Global Public Relations; became an activist, author and peace podcast host, www.peacepodcast.org; you are the co-founder of the Rotary E-Club of World Peace and you were also elected as President of the Rotary E-Club of World Peace, www.rotaryeclubofworldpeace.org; you were also elected as President of the United Nations Association - Santa Barbara, www.unasb.org; you received the Spirit of the United Nations award; you received a Lifetime Achievement Award from The Visioneers International Network; you received The Awakening Peace Award - and more! Barbara, you are living proof that it only takes one person to make a *huge* difference in the world. Thank you for all you do and are, and most of all, thank you for your friendship.

Deborah Burke Henderson (testimonial, superb editor, subtitle and back cover brainstormer, support network and major cheerleader) - Thank you, Deborah (and Devorah) for your editing expertise, outstanding suggestions, wisdom, insights, humor, support, counseling, consulting, cheerleading, insightful testimonial, and most of all, for your friendship. Your life story embodies courage, determination, strength and love and I can feel these qualities in everything you are and do. Whether you are creating a custom-made gift for a family member or friend, submitting a story about someone special for a newspaper article, writing a delightful children's story, creating a new Haiku, taking a sensory walk amid the healing beauty of nature - everything you do comes from the heart of love. You have given so much of yourself to me, Deborah, and I am touched beyond all adequate words except to say a profound and loving "thank you." I don't know how you found the time to help me in the middle of your own full, creative and spiritual life, but as I keep saying, it only takes one person to vibrate the soul of peace. Thank you, my friend.

Arthur P. Ciaramicoli, Ed.D., Ph.D. (testimonial and contributor) - Thank you for reading *Peace Dreamer* and for writing such a meaningful testimonial in the middle of your own busy professional life as a clinical psychologist, dynamic speaker and prolific writer. I also appreciate your input on possible subtitles for *Peace Dreamer*. Most of all, thank you for all the work you do to make the world more aware of the importance of empathy, diversity celebration and human understanding. All the books you have written raise human consciousness to a higher level and they include *The Triumph of Diversity: Rejoice in and Benefit from the Interconnectedness of Humankind; The Power of Empathy: A Practical Guide to Creating Intimacy, Self-Understanding and Lasting Love; The Soulful Leader: Success with Authenticity, Integrity and Empathy.* Thank you, Arthur. www.balanceyoursuccess.com

Bernie S. Siegel, M.D. (testimonial) - Thank you for writing such a powerful testimonial on behalf of *Peace Dreamer*. You were modest to mention only two books as part of your brief bio. I just counted all the books on your website, and to my amazement, there are 19 floating around our universe - including the New York Times best-selling book that has been in my home for years - *Love, Medicine & Miracles*. Your work as a wellness and spiritual leader continue to grace our world. For your big heart, innovative thinking, use of the creative arts in healing your patients, the Exceptional Cancer Patients Therapy program, and now The Art of Healing Support Group for anyone experiencing health challenges - thank you. The Visioneers International Network Hero of Humanity Award is well-deserved, Bernie. www.berniesiegelmd.com

Liseli Fitzpatrick, Ph.D. (testimonial, brainstormer of the subtitle of *Peace Dreamer,* and contributor of the original poem, "we've been here before") - When I heard you speak at Open Spirit, my heart melted. The eloquence in which you spoke about peace, the earth, African philosophy and love touched me to my core, and I knew I had to reach out to you. You are the embodiment of *Peace Dreamer*. During your keynote speech, you also read an original poem that brought tears to my eyes and pain in my soul. I had to include "we've been here before" in this book. People need to read this poem and be awakened by it. Not only are you an exquisite poet and speaker, you are also making a difference in your role as professor of African Diasporic Cosmologies and Sacred Ontologies in the Department of African Studies at Wellesley College. Thank you for blessing my book with your unique and loving vibration, Liseli. www.wellesley.edu/africana/faculty/fitzpatrick

Reverend Dr. Deborah L. Clark (testimonial) - I needed your special blessing to launch *Peace Dreamer*, Reverend Debbie. Thank you for writing such a glowing testimonial. In Open Spirit: A Place of Hope, Health and Harmony, I love witnessing the way you bring people together from every walk of life. In your calm, wise and loving way, you are a light amid all the darkness and I can't thank you enough for all you do. You embody the essence of peace as pastor of Edwards Church, as the multi-faith coordinator of Open Spirit, as the author of *Ice Cream at the Ashram: Holy Journey, Holy River, Holy Week*, in your love for your spouse, Fran Bogle, in your delight and love for your standard poodle, Jeannie, in your devotion to veterans through the various programs you offer at Open Spirit, in your yoga and meditation expertise, and in the spiritual counseling you generously offer anyone who reaches out to you. For all this and more, thank you. www.openspiritcenter.org

Jan Krause Greene (testimonial) - To my longtime friend, author of *I Call Myself Earth Girl, What Happens in the Space Between* and *Left for Dead: From Surviving to Thriving*, peace activist, environmentalist, lover of the earth, tree hugger, innovative educator, rock collector, imaginative writer, spellbinding storyteller, gifted actress and devoted grandmother - thank you for making time in your busy schedule to read *Peace Dreamer* and for creating a deeply meaningful testimonial on its behalf. You are one incredible human being and one incredible friend, Jan. www.jkgreene.com

Maya Rosenbloom (contributor) - To my brilliant, deep, creative seven-year-old granddaughter. Thank you, Maya, for sharing your beautiful wisdom and heart in *Peace Dreamer*. Your idea about "kindness arguments" will teach grown-ups how to shift their hearts towards kindness and love in the middle of an argument. It will also teach grown-ups how to care about the well-being of others. These are lessons many of us still need to learn and thank you for helping us. I love our deep talks together, Maya, and I also love you wayyy beyond the moon and back. Thank you for being a beautiful example of "peace begins with me."

Eden Schwartz (contributor) - my dearest sister. Thank you for your beautiful words of wisdom about nature and its power to heal us. Because you are the essence of "peace begins with me," I always love to include a part of your special vibration in my books. Your generous heart, the way you give your unconditional love to your family and friends, the way you shine love, stand for love and are love, and the way you care about peace, kindness and diversity celebration, make me profoundly grateful that you and I are sisters and friends. Thank you for always being such a strong support network for me, Eden. I love you.

The *Shift of Heart* Facebook Community (contributors) - A special thank you to Laurel, Faith, Autumn, Alice, Cynthia, Jean and Diane for sharing your personal stories of inner growth, healing and transformation. When you decided to share such a deep part of who yourself with the world, it took faith, trust and courage. Thank you! Your openness will help many people along the way.

Thank you to all the members of the *Shift of Heart* community who represent the kind of world I have always envisioned. I deeply appreciate the wisdom and positive vibrations you share on our online community pages as well as throughout the pages of *Peace Dreamer*. Thank you for being such an important part of my life. Our circle of love, peace, healing and hope is deep and real.

Veronica Yager (Book Designer) - The incredible ease I felt in working with you is an innate quality that can't be taught in school. I am grateful for your expertise, experience and professionalism, and along with these important aspects, I am deeply grateful for your patience, positive and calm attitude, outstanding communication style, work ethic and friendship. You have made *Peace Dreamer* shine in its light in every way. www.YellowStudiosOnline.com

Barry Rosenbloom (stellar editor, back cover brainstormer, and incredible support network) - Thank you, my love. Thank you for reading *Peace Dreamer* and for making insightful suggestions and edits. "Eagle Eye" did it again! After all these years, there are new things about you that I am still discovering and appreciating more than ever - the way you revere our earth and all of nature, all your problem-solving skills, handyman expertise, innate talents (I still think you are an undiscovered artist), your passion for fishing and your philosophy of "catch and release," your determination and resilience, and your ability to open your heart to giving and receiving love. I am deeply grateful that our paths crossed over 50 years ago. *I love you.*

With a Grateful Heart

"Life without love is like a tree without blossoms or fruit."

– Kahlil Gibran

Many of us are descendants of immigrants. Gratefully, I am no exception. I owe who I am today to my ancestors and am lovingly taking this opportunity to thank my grandfathers, Hyman and Harry, my grandmothers, Sarah and Ida, their families, and all the families before them. My grandmothers and grandfathers came to America without any money, and yet despite unbelievable hardships, they found a way to make a life here. Would I have had the same resilience? The same problem-solving skills? The same ability to live without my comforts while still believing in a dream for a better life? I'm not sure, and yet somewhere in my DNA, I can sense their determination, resilience, problem-solving skills and starry-eyed dreams within me, too.

I am also grateful to my two loving parents, Ruth and Joseph, who encouraged my unique qualities to shine; my beautiful sister, Eden; my amazing husband, Barry, who works with me in creating a relationship that has as its mantras, *never give up, I love you, I see you, I hear you, I forgive you, onward and upward*; my son, Jeremy and my daughter Jodie - *I love you*; my incredible daughter-in-law, Emily; her amazing parents, Susan and Neil; my granddaughters, Maya and Eva, who make me giggle and laugh every day; my awesome brother-in-law,

Abe; my heart-centered niece, Tara; my caring nephews, Jared and Aaron; my supportive cousins, Dara and Michelle; my cherished friends - thank you for being part of my extended family of support, love and light.

One more "thank you." To you. My reader. My new friend. It is worth saying these words again from the deepest part of my heart to yours ...

Thank you for joining me in being the love, compassion and kindness our world needs. Thank you for shining your life's compass towards peace. Never give up on our collective dream.

Step by step, resolve to do the inner work needed to heal yourself, and breath by breath, visualize a world that stands tall for love, equality, justice, diversity celebration, and hope.

About the Author

Cheryl Melody Baskin is an author, playwright, peace educator, intuitive life coach, musician, motivational speaker and sound healer.

Her books and plays include *Peace Dreamer: A Journey of Hope in Bad Times and Good, Heart-Dreamer: Stepping into Life, Love, Creativity and Dreams - No Matter What, Shift of Heart: Paths to Healing and Love,* and *Peace Begins with You and Me - A Musical Play with Life-Changing Messages for Every Generation.*

As a musician, she is a performing artist and has nine award-winning albums with positive messages for both adults and children. She is also the founder, moderator and intuitive life coach of "Shift of Heart," a large and inclusive Facebook community of love, support and hope.

"Melody" enjoys a balance of quiet contemplation, meaningful social interaction, dreaming new dreams, and the healing power of nature. She is also a strong believer in peace, diversity celebration, listening to life's wisdom whispers, trusting in the magical mystery of the unknown, healing from inside-out, and walking the path of love.

Cheryl Melody Baskin was recently honored with a Lifetime Achievement Award from The Visioneers International Network.

Contact Information

Website: www.cherylmelody.com
Email: cherylmelody@gmail.com

***Shift of Heart* Facebook Community:**
https://www.facebook.com/groups/103850356767217/

Books and Plays:
- *Peace Dreamer: A Journey of Hope in Bad Times and Good*
- *Heart-Dreamer: Stepping into Life, Love, Creativity and Dreams - No Matter What*
- *Peace Begins with You and Me: A Musical Play with Life-Changing Messages for Every Generation*
- *Shift of Heart: Paths to Healing and Love*

"One Planet"
https://www.youtube.com/watch?v=ClvTg7rmn0o

Cheryl Melody's Music:
https://itunes.apple.com/us/artist/cheryl-melody/4106045
https://www.amazon.com/Cheryl-Melody/e/B000AP8QPQ

Books and Music by Cheryl Melody Baskin, LLC

Permissions

Sincere gratitude to all those who generously gave me permission to include their words in *Peace Dreamer*.

Liseli A. Fitzpatrick, Ph.D. - Trinidadian poet, "we've been here before" (The 1619 Project), https://aboutplacejournal.org/issues/works-of-resistance-resilience/in-the-spirit-of-resilience/liseli-a-fitzpatrick/

Dr. Desmond Berghofer - Author, *The Visioneers: A Courage Story about Belief in the Future*. Co-Founder: The Visioneers International Network, www.thevisioneers.ca

Dr. Geraldine Schwartz - Author, *Journeys of Second Adulthood*. Founder, Vancouver Learning Centre. www.vancouverlearningcentre.org; Co-Founder: The Visioneers International Network, www.thevisioneers.ca

Dr. Robert Muller - Former United Nations Assistant Secretary-General. Author, *Most of All They Taught Me Happiness* and *7500 Hundred Ideas for a Better World*. Creator of the United Nations *World Core Curriculum*. www.robertmuller.org; http://goodmorningworld.org

Barbara Gaughen-Muller - Co-Author: *7500 Ideas for a Better World*; *Revolutionary Conversations: The Tools You Need for the Success You Want*. President - UNA-USA Santa Barbara, www.unasb.org; President - www.rotaryeclubofworldpeace.org; www.peacepodcast.org

Arthur P. Ciaramicoli, Ed.D., Ph.D. - Author, *The Triumph of Diversity*; *The Stress Solution; The Power of Empathy.* Clinical psychologist. www.BalanceYourSuccess.com

Fred Rogers - Creator and host of "Mr. Rogers' Neighborhood," musician and minister. (Quote by Fred Rogers provided courtesy of the Fred Rogers Company). www.fredrogers.org

Ram Dass - Spiritual teacher and author of *Be Here Now.* www.RamDass.org

Leo Buscaglia - Author, professor, speaker. Citation. Reprinted from permission of SLACK Incorporated. *Living, Loving & Learning.* Thorofare, NJ. Slack, Incorporated, 1982.

David Whyte - Poet and author of *The Heart Aroused: Poetry and the Preservation of the Soul in Corporate America.* www.davidwhyte.com

Made in the USA
Middletown, DE
18 March 2021